Letters from Lillian

Faith and Practice

among
Modern Liberal Quakers

Elizabeth F. Boardman

2011

Purchase from Amazon
Direct inquiries to *eboardman@sbcglobal.net*

Back cover photo by Arthur Koch.

Acknowledgements

Early drafts were read by generous readers with red pen in hand. Non-Quakers claimed to learn a lot; members of the Religious Society of Friends could think of even more to tell. Every reader helped.

So, many thanks to Jane Berger, Emily Boardman, Faith Childs, Kate Dawe, Pat Jones, Jerry Fishman, Kathy Hyzy, Fran Peavey, Shirley Sullivan and Gloria Valoris. Hope this final version will please, inform, and stimulate.

Table of Contents

Introduction

My name is Marla Salas. In 2008, on sabbatical from teaching in the humanities department of a small college and recovering from an ended romance, I went to work in Pakistan for a year, in a school for the deaf.

Preparing for the trip, I got in touch with my old college room-mate, Lillian Canner, who had lived in Karachi when we first got out of school. We expected to exchange letters about Islamic society, but ended up writing mostly about "silent meeting Friends" in the United States.

That came about because one of my house mates in Karachi, a young man from Arizona, was a Quaker, and so was Lillian. I got curious about what their faith was all about. Were they Christians? Theists? How do they operate a congregation without a pastor? Can anyone join a Friends Meeting? People of any race? What about gays?

*The house in Karachi was like an old-fashioned guest house,
where everyone was served supper at a big table. I often
found myself sitting with Jeremy, and after exchanging the
news of the day, I asked him such questions about Friends,
and then checked out his responses with Lily by e-mail.
What is meant by "testing a leading? What are "Friends
testimonies"? Are all Quakers pacifists? What is a war tax
resister? How are children and teens treated among
Friends? What about the elderly and the dying? Lily wrote
extensive answers and slowly the idea of a book began to
emerge in my mind.*

*Meanwhile, Jeremy was an enigma to me for a long while.
And I wondered about the father he was always talking
about. Lily began to wonder, too. Slowly we both got
answers and inspiration.*

Marla, Lillian, Jeremy and the other characters in this
story, though intended to resemble real people, are
fictional. Some of the place names are imaginary. But
the Quaker practices and dilemmas described here are
absolutely true to life.

~~~~~~

Marla's "leading"

Oh, dear Marla, I feel that you've gone to the ends of the earth and you probably haven't even left your friends in London yet. You may not get e-mail for weeks. I am sending this by e and snail mail, both.

I am glad you have this opportunity to truck off to an exotic land, to follow a strong "leading" (as we Quakers would say). I'm proud that you will do work that is close to your heart among the Islamic people -- whom some these days call "enemy."

I assume your sister etc were able to see you off from the Tucson airport. Did they pour champagne and throw rose petals? Did anyone from the Society for the Blind come with final instructions or packages for you to carry? Do you have extra things you have to carry and keep track of during your visit in London?

Never mind -- by the time you read this letter, weeks will have passed and memories of your departure day will be lost in a swirl of new impressions and accommodations. I can imagine and even remember how it is, though it has been thirty years since I lived in Pakistan myself.

Do write when you get a chance, and tell me all about it. I hope you'll get a computer or at least access to one, right away. I wonder if your office computers will write in Urdu as well as English.

Anyway, my dear, I am wishing you all kinds of blessings in your new land, and I look forward to anything you can find time to write.

Cheers.................................Lillian

~~~~~~

Pakistan

Marla, probably you have not even arrived in Pakistan from London yet, but I want you to be greeted by letters from home when you do get there.

Also, thinking of you in Karachi puts me into a sort of time warp, remembering aspects of my own time there so long ago, in the early sixties. You'll have to tell me how it is now. Is there still a threat of malaria? Do you have to take those horrible-tasting big quinine pills? Does the traffic still stay to the left, as in Great Britain? They used to say that the camels couldn't be taught to change to the right side of the road. Are there still camel carts every where?

Flashbacks! The hardest thing for me was having servants. My husband and I were virtually poor at that time, but in Pakistan we suddenly were seen as Americans of "social status." I definitely resisted the idea.

But eight servants had already been engaged for us by the Ford Foundation. They were literally standing in a line at the front door when we arrived, like some scene from the days of the British Raj. Counting their spouses and children, we had 32 dependents. Scary!

I was twenty-one years old, and there was just me, my husband, and one baby. Did we really need all these helpers? My puritanical mother had always taught me that "a good woman does her own work." So how could I be asking these other people, half of them twice my age, to do it for me?

How could I play the superior role of "memsahib" when my Quaker faith instructed that "there is that of God in every person" and all are equal?

In the beginning, I often got into trouble bucking the local culture, paying the servants "too much," treating them with respect, refusing to lock up all the household cupboards, and arguing about all these things with other memsahibs, both Pakistani and expatriate. Slowly, slowly I adapted to the local culture. Finally I came to understand that paying others to work in our home was a way of sharing our relative wealth.

Maybe in your shared housing situation, with more household equipment, and you being sixty instead of 21, the issue will not be as difficult. I am eager to hear how it goes. Karachi isn't anywhere near the Taliban battle zones, but there may be various kinds of chaos and danger. Do tell – and keep safe.

Back here at home, I am taking full advantage of being retired from paid work. I am still "doing my own work," including stripping and refinishing my little deck, despite the aches and pains it causes me. It is well worth the effort. Amazing how a rich brown color can change the aspect of wood so that it seems elegant instead of utilitarian. I'll finish the stairs tomorrow.

Cheers..............................Lily

~~~~~~

Ecology

Dear Marla,

I am eager to hear whenever your e-mail is up and

running. Meanwhile, I think I should batch some of these little letters together to save on postage and "global footprint." Am I being compulsive? You should see how I parse out water, using the smallest amount possible and recycling it all in to my scruffy little flower pots and on to the tiny vegetable garden.
  Lately I lie awake nights wondering how I could get the city to change its rules forbidding the "grey water" from sinks and washing machines from going onto lawns and into flower beds. Could I find a plumber who would shift my drains out to the back yard? Would that be an act of "civil disobedience" – you know, breaking the law of the land in deference to the laws of the Divine?

I think there is a bit of gentle unacknowledged competition among Quakers at my Meeting (church) to see who can be the most ecologically correct. We try to use less water, less electricity, less gas and gasoline, less imported foods and goods than others. I suppose among forms of competition, it is the healthiest!

Now I am thinking of taking a train, instead of driving, when I go across the country in the summer. I am not really sure it will be more ecological than flying, given that the trains are not (yet) full of passengers. But I want to model and encourage more use of trains so that it becomes a prime way of travel in the future.

Anyway, penurious though I am of water and power, my little house and my straggly garden are pleasing me very much these days. I can have the doors and windows open all day as I write in here. The light and air counteract the ugly mechanical hum of the computer. I love hearing the voices of neighbor children, and the special rumble and click of the skateboards that two of the older boys practice on for hours at a time.

"The land is sweet and good."

Cheers…………………..Lil

I answered these three all at once, while I was settling in. My situation was certainly nothing like Lillian's of thirty years ago. Here's how she responded, effusive and full of unlikely references to her "Meeting for Worship," as she calls her church.

~~~~~~

Marla's situation in Karachi

Dear wonderful Marla,

I got your first e-mail yesterday and it was great to hear from you. I'll stop sending hard copy, too. Wow, in the sixties it took at least ten days for even an air mail letter to reach Karachi, and then another ten days for the return letter. By Internet, it'll take only a few hours, depending on when we get time to answer.

I am so glad that the cooperative "guest house" and arrangements are comfortable for you, and that you've got the "glass half full" perspective to see it that way. Sounds like a scenario from the old colonial days when Britishers came to work in Pakistan without their families. How great that you have two rooms to yourself, and don't have to shop or cook.

I should have realized that the servant situation would be very different for you there where the International House is in charge of the grounds keeper and the driver. Even the cook, it sounds like.

I am glad to hear that you and the other staff at the school for the blind are eating lunch right with the clients, the same food and everything. It dramatizes your respect for them and your sense of equality despite their inability to see. But I hope you get a break or two in the course of the day.

It is hard for me to picture how you do your work without sharing a language with your clients, but then I remember that even in Tucson, often the people you worked with did not really know English very well. You are some kind of hero, girl -- or maybe "angel" has a less macho ring to it!

The poignant things you said about missing your little pooch got me thinking right in the middle of the silent Meeting for Worship today about dogs and compassion.

Quakers intend to seek always for the divine in other humans. Dogs don't have to seek it, do they -- they just see it immediately! Everyone is divine to them – rich or poor, black or white, gay or straight! No layers of judgment to peel away.

Maybe a dog has to check out the odors on a person, and of course dogs have to protect their owners. But otherwise they are ready to lick, like, play with or save you, even if you are a stranger. Plodding out into the snow with the reviving cask of whiskey around the neck. Rushing in to the burning building to save the baby. Barking like mad to rouse you in the smoke-filled room. Compassion incarnate! What other animal responds to human needs this way?

Is compassion an evolutionary trait? Clearly it has physiological aspects – think how your heart literally swells, adrenaline rushes, tears fall when you are moved by compassion. How does this stuff work?

If any understanding had come clear to me, I might have risen to speak of it in Meeting. But as you can see, I remain even now in a muddle of awe and wonder.

There is so much I will never have time to learn about the world.

Write again – I love hearing from you.

Your friend.......................Lily

I wasn't thinking about compassionate dogs at this point but about how to respond in a compassionate but reasonable way to all the beggars on the route between the guest house and the school. So I wrote to Lily about that.

~~~~~~

Beggars

Dear Marla,

I do indeed remember the Karachi beggars. Scruffy clothes, whiny voices, dirty hands extended: *Bakshish, memsahib! Bakshish!*

In those days, some of the beggars, we were told, had been deliberately blinded or maimed, and they were made to take any *bakshish* they collected back to their enslavers in the secret corners of the bazaar. So we used to give food instead.

Do you think that still goes on? I sure hope organizations like the one you are working for have had an effect.

What about back in Tucson, another attractively warm place, are there beggars there? We have many here in Santa Carla. Since I started using public transportation and walk so much, I've made friends with one or two that I see often. In an important way, they share my values. Can I share a little bit I wrote recently?

I got Charlie to tell me a bit about his life. He is often playing a dulcimer in the 16th Street Station, where he presents himself as a long-haired hippy with glasses and a colorful headband. He's been to college and had a variety of jobs, but he doesn't like ambition or consumerism. "Hey," he tells me, "even when you win the rat race, aren't you still a rat?" He is a devotee of Meher Baba and Urantia. He says his brother makes eighty grand a year, but has sold his soul to do it. ...

Charlie wrote a little piece for me – here is part of it.

"It is noteworthy that I am a finder of treasures through merely strolling about town, and that my real trippy girlfriend is a purveyor of curiosities to all who share in the magic of San Francisco. When I first started playing in the early '90s, I was known as Birdman, because there was a parakeet tethered to my shoulder while I strummed my dulcimer and it sang along. And that little bird would make twice as much as me..."

Charlie says that he asks about a hundred passers-by for every one "tip" he receives. White men in suits never give him anything, he says, but excluding them, men and women drop coins and bills into his dulcimer case equally often, with middle-aged white women the most likely to give a big bill People rushing to and from work don't often stop. His dulcimer attracts some attention, especially from out-of-towners, and once a group of stoned dead-heads gave him $54.

Do you think the Islamic mandate to give regularly to the poor, I think it is called *zakat* -- do you think it means that there are more beggars in Karachi, and that they get "tips" from more than "one out of a hundred," as Charlie reports in Santa Carla?

City life is rich and intense in a variety of ways the world over, huh?

Love.........................Lillian

I was preoccupied and busy sorting out my new life and I go t another letter from Lillian about beggars before I could answer the first.

~~~~~~

Sweet panhandler

Marla, do you know the Faure <u>Requiem</u>? I listen to it at home a lot, and last night I heard it at Symphony Hall. I think of it as a predictable tear-jerker. When I want to grieve out my sorrow for the world, I can always get myself weeping by listening to this Requiem, even in public. (I was discreet; no one could tell.) Nothing like a good cry to make a girl feel better.

Encountered a little angel on the way home, another of my begging buddies. Following the crowds from the Symphony Hall to the subway, I could see dozens of well-heeled people passing by Terry, who was kneeling as usual at the bottom of the escalator in his filthy clothes with his toothless grin. By the time I reached him, I was popping with indignation and pulling a dollar out of my purse.

"All those rich people passed you, and no one gave you a thing!" I exclaimed.

Terry just smiled sweetly. "They don't owe me anything."

Golly.

So back to you, is it comfortable for you to be sharing dinner with all those other people every day? How many are there? I guess they are all working at service organizations of some sort, right? Do they all live at the guest house there with you?

Must be nice not to have to shop, cook, or clean up. Unless that deprives you of opportunities to go to the wonderful markets.

Tell more.

Love………………………..Lily

War taxes

Hi, Marla, I am writing to you to put off the moment when I must compose my annual protest letter about war taxes to the Internal Revenue Service. I haven't told you earlier that I am a war tax resister – hope you are not dismayed to hear it.

The thing is that at least half of our tax dollars nowadays go to support the Department of Defense, and that doesn't even include most of the cost of the wars in Iraq and Afghanistan, which get "supplemental" funds. It really causes me anguish to see so much of my own federal tax money used to pay for killing other people and destroying their homelands.

Some Quakers openly refuse to send the war portion when they file their IRS 1040, even though that is breaking the law. Some don't pay at all. We think of it as civil disobedience, obeying a "higher" law.

Usually the government gets the money eventually, along with interest charges and penalties, but at least we didn't pay voluntarily. Other people make an even greater sacrifice by "living below the line," deliberately earning so little money that they don't owe any taxes.

But I'm like the ordinary Joe; most of my taxes are withheld from my pay check, and the government gets to spend half of it on war long before I even file my IRS Form 1040. I don't like it.

So the letter I'm resolved to send today will tell the IRS, with copies to my legislators, that I am **paying under protest.** Yeh, like that, in bold.

But I am still paying. Darn. Not much, but enough for a big gun of some sort. A gun whose bullets might pierce the heart of some innocent Afghani woman who just happens to step forward into the line of fire as she moves towards a display of grapes in the bazaar ....leaving her child screaming and sobbing over her body ....leaving the young American who pulled the trigger horrified and plagued for years with bad dreams...

Oh, darley, tell me to stop. Sorry....Maybe I shouldn't send this letter....Why not?....Dear mankind......

Dear Marla, I am so glad you are not posted to Quetta – it is too close for comfort to Afghanistan.

Love and sorrow.........................Lil

Good heavens, I surely did not expect all this radical stuff from Lillian. I thought Quakers were quiet mousy people in grey clothes who prayed in silent and did good deeds for the poor. I asked someone about it at supper and learned that the young American man who works on paratransit services here is a Quaker. So maybe I'll get with him to learn more.

General questions about Quakers

Hi, Marla, thanks so much for your letter all full of questions about Quakers. You should ask the same questions of this Jeremy Anderson you have met. We Quakers have quite a range of opinions about everything! Is he from a Friends Church (with a preacher and a Protestant sort of church service) or from an unprogrammed Friends Meeting, like me?

Here are some off-the-cuff answers from me.

- Yes, many Quakers choose to work in service jobs, paid or volunteer, in poor neighborhoods and third world countries.
- No, such overseas service is not a requirement of membership as it seems to be with the Seventh Day Adventists (or is it the Mormons?)
- Yes, there are degrees of membership among Quakers in the sense that some people call themselves Quakers even if they do not belong to a local Meeting. Or, though listed as members, they do not participate regularly. I think it is fair to say that a full-fledged Quaker attends worship virtually every Sunday, attends Business Meeting once a month, and serves on at least one committee!
- No, you don't have to be born into a Quaker family to become one. In fact, most Quakers are

"convinced," not "birthright." There is a thoughtful membership application process.

- Yes, most Quakers are pacifists, meaning that they aim to live up to the "testimony" of nonviolence and not to participate in or support war, capital punishment, personal weapons, or physical abuse of any kind.
- And no, I don't know for sure where Islam stands on the subject of nonviolence, though I do believe that Muslims are far less war-like than westerners like to think, especially these days!

Tell more about Jeremy. Is he working for the same organization you are? What other Americans and Europeans are around? Do you have the opportunity to make friends with local Pakistanis?

Being a "full-fledged Quaker" myself, I must rush off to a Peace and Social Concerns Committee meeting now.

Til soon.........................Lil

~~~~~~

Sending Faith and Practice

Greetings, dear friend,

It is intriguing to see you more preoccupied with Quaker faith than with Islam even while you are immersed in Muslim culture. But of course for yourself, raised in a Christian culture, Quaker ideas resonate more quickly than the Islamic ones.

If only Quakers could have a call to prayer like the *muzzeins* you must be hearing at least five times daily there in Karachi! I loved them, even the modern version, all amplified and maybe even recorded and on a timer. I also much appreciate the fact that such a great proportion of the men in Islamic countries participate in the prayers. I love their shoulder to shoulder stance, and their willingness to kneel down, head to the floor, butt in the air. What position could be more humble? Humility is a virtue mostly lost in America, don't you think?

Often I have wished I could kneel like a repentant Catholic. Or lie spread-eagle on my back on the floor. Perhaps that is a throw-back to my childhood days on the lawn under the horse-chestnut tree, when the glittering blue sky way up beyond the branches was said to hold heaven and God –or maybe even Superman! Wasn't that "worship" in a kid?

But adult Quakers in Meeting for Worship generally sit quite proper and straight-backed on chairs or benches, mostly with heads down and eyes closed – did Jeremy tell you? But the chairs are often in a circle, the room is plain and often filled with light, we wear casual, comfortable clothes and shoes. It is a lovely silence to share with others for an hour.

It is from within that silence that a person may feel called to stand and speak, or even sing. Anyone can. At our best, we speak briefly, audibly, from our own deep experience. We listen with an open mind and heart, *"in expectant waiting for the promptings of the Divine Spirit."*

That line is from our basic guide book, the *Faith and Practice.* Since you are exploring Quakerism with such enthusiasm, I will send you a copy. It includes the gems of earlier Quaker writings, an outline of our organizations and procedures, and most important, a listing of our testimonies, with the "queries and advices" which help us live up to the testimonies. All of our "practices" arise from our "faith" in the Divine spirit and its presence in every person on the planet.

By the way, every yearly meeting has its own version of *Faith and Practice,* so Jeremy's might be somewhat different from mine. Pacific Yearly Meeting covers only California, Nevada and Hawaii.

More on all this later, my dear. Keep on writing – I love hearing from you.

Cheers...................Lily

I did keep writing, but I couldn't keep up with Lily's pace. She seems to like writing about Quakers, so why not? I kept asking questions.

~~~~~~

Meeting for Worship

Good, Marla, I'm glad that Jeremy told you more about
Meeting for Worship, about coming into the quiet circle
of chairs, children, too, smiling around at people, then
sinking down into the silence. Having done it for
decades, I forget that it is an amazing experience for
newcomers, even people who are used to meditating on
their own. There is such a sense of affirmation for the
process because others are doing it all around you, first
quieting the body and then the mind, letting go of ego,
moving into a state of expectant waiting for "the still,
small voice of God."

In my Meeting, the children don't stay more than
fifteen minutes or so, but you can see how they settle
down into quietness, too, before they go off for their
First Day School classes. At the end of the hour, they
join us again for refreshments, and for announcements
about all the other activities that go on among us.

I can just hear you asking: What activities? It is
different from one Meeting to another, but there are
things like book discussion groups, hymn singing
(separate from the worship), young adult Friends
gatherings, adult religious education, Bible study,
maybe a mid-week worship, and of course committee
meetings and business meetings. There are
welcomings and weddings and memorial services.

Also after Worship, any up-coming regional meetings

are announced and visitors get to introduce themselves. Then the clerk says something like, "Meeting will rise," and we all go off for coffee and snacks and visiting with each other. It's good. You know where you belong when you hang out with a group of like-minded people week after week.

Writing this out, including mention of the hymns, reminds me that I am supposed to call the piano tuner for the ancient piano at Meeting. So I'm out of here for now!

Cheers.......................Lillian

~~~~~~

Social groups

Marla, you are not getting all romantic, are you, about this Jeremy you say you are meeting almost daily? I fear that your tender heart will get bruised again.

But perhaps I leap to wrong conclusions. It is good to hear of the little cadre of non-profit service organizations that has developed there in Karachi – there was nothing like that thirty years ago. If Jeremy's outfit is doing paratransit services among other things, I wonder if he knows John Richards, the Santa Carla Quaker who has worked on transit for the disabled in so many countries. (I don't think John had a project in Karachi, though.)

To answer your query, yes, I am still plugging away at the book about my women's group of twenty years. But it is not going well. I have to change everyone's identity, of course, and even disguise our surroundings. I am a good reporter of real fact, not so good at creating fiction or developing character. But I am slogging away at it, because I think women's groups are an important invisible component of our society which deserves to be acknowledged. I can't think how I'd have survived without mine.

Many of the people in my Meeting share in the intense community life there, and know some about my spiritual development and my activism. But they know almost nothing about my grown children, my work, or my love life. It is my female friends (and one or two gay friends, too) who know a lot about my life.

I am glad for women friend of my own age and stage. Including you!

Cheers.................Lily

Well, I had to answer that one! Here's part of what I wrote:

> *Lillian, no way am I "getting all romantic" about Jeremy Anderson! He could be my son, he's so young. Can't be more than 35. Guess my glowing remarks about his thoughtful ideas and "centered" personality led you to misconstrue the nature of my admiration. And anyway, you know I am here partly*

to get over my disappointment in the last man I
"admired, and I am in no hurry to fall for anyone
again, even though I am not such a committed
celibate as you claim to be.

Also, Lily, I'm not sure Jeremy would have romantic
inclinations towards any woman. He is very good
looking, but reserved and slight -- and single still. I
haven't asked him about that, but between you and
me, I've wondered if he might be gay. That would
help explain why he is so easy for me to talk with --
there's none of that sexually-laden banter that usually
gets into straight male-female conversation. But
maybe it's just that I am old enough to be his mother!

Lily's response came by e-mail the next day.

Dear Marla,

Well, good, if Jeremy is gay, that might make him an
 especially good friend. No wife or girlfriend around to

feel nervous about you being friends with him. Plus, it
is always great to have friends much younger and older
than oneself. Enjoy his company!

Gotta run.

Love...................Lil

~~~~~~

Non-Christian Quakers

Dear Marla,

Gosh, girl, you ask good questions. "How can Jeremy be a Quaker when he says he is not a Christian?"

You need to ask Jeremy about his own experience. But it is true that, although we are deeply grounded in Christian faith, a Friends Meeting does not require that its members adhere to a single tight definition of what it means to be a Christian. Rather, we are to "wrestle with Christianity." We are to be seekers of the truth. And we are to acknowledge the truth to be a moving target; we speak of "continuing revelation."

I have not called myself a Christian for many years because I do not believe in the mythological stories of Christianity. Perhaps I should say, they are not useful to me. It has never been important to me to believe in the virgin birth or the physical resurrection of Jesus. I think of Jesus as being the first who taught that there is a divine element, not just in himself, but in every person. This is the quintessential Quaker concept.

Also, nowadays, some Friends hesitate to call themselves Christian because, alas, Christianity has become identified with rigid and unforgiving attitudes towards all who have not "taken Christ as their personal savior," all who do not adhere to a single interpretation of scripture. That is not an attitude that tolerant, ecumenical Quakers share.

Still, most Quakers have been raised in a Christian culture and follow the Judeo-Christian code of ethics. Though I am in no way a conventional Christian, I am proud to call myself a serious, 24/7 follower of Jesus of Nazareth. You know: that radical guy who questioned the Establishment of his day! I think this kind of designation works for many other Quakers, too. Ask Jeremy.

Thanks for these questions, Marla! People don't usually ask like this, and I am almost shy about answering. Thanks for encouraging me to "speak my truth."

Love…………..Lily

PS.   I sent the *Faith and Practice* about a week ago.

PPS So Jeremy does know John Richard! The Quaker world is very small. Probably the world of paratransit advocates is very small, too.

Weeding

Marla, sorry I haven't written for a while. After weeks of cold and rain, I've taken advantage these last few sunny days for spring cleaning and gardening. My joints are sore, my stomach muscles are strained, my hands and arms are all scratched up – and my place looks good. I am tanned and happy!

The only part I hate is the weeding. I don't mind getting down on my knees -- I think it is good for the soul and the ego. But I hate the inevitable metaphors about human life.

It is not true what the garden pundits say, that you can crowd out the weeds with good plants. In my garden, weeds grow especially well among and on top of the "good" plants, where it is especially hard to get at them. Evil is totally intertwined with good, and the weeds will inherit the earth! (I've been reading a wonderful new book from the New York Times Bestseller list by Alan Weisman about this: *The World Without Us*.)

I'm glad you are getting out and about to see the sights in Karachi and nearby. I remember the beach very well – we went there every week except during the dangerous monsoon months. We passed through a wonderfully stinky fishmongers' neighborhood on the way – I wonder if it is still there.

But I don't remember any museum in Karachi and am interested to hear that there is an art and history museum now. You'll be getting to the ancient ruins at Mohenjodaro one of these days, I suppose. It is so hard to maintain perspective about our little lives. Historic places like Mohenjodaro and books like Weisman's help. Enjoy!

Cheers.........................Lily Ann

By this point, Lily and I were into "parallel play," you might call it, each of us writing most about our own activities in the two radically different worlds we inhabited. She commented on my reports and vice versa, but more and more, I encouraged her to tell me about her Quaker life. I began to see that her descriptions might work for a larger audience than just me.

~~~~~~

Children's Day preparation

Dear Marla,

Just a quickie – too much to do. Among other things, I am the designated coordinator for the Meeting's annual Children's Day, and it is coming up shortly.

In some places, a new baby gets a personal welcoming or blessing from the Meeting, but here, we have invented a once-a-year event celebrating all the children at once. It takes about 30 minutes (to match the attention span of a little one), after taking me about four to five hours over several weeks to organize!

We give a plaque to small people who have turned six during the preceding year. It features a line from our forefather, William Penn, which reads, *"Let us then see*

what love can do." I'm always hoping the kids will still
have it and display it when they get to college, and will
be asked where they got it and who William Penn was.

We give a Bible to people who have turned twelve.
Both plaque and Bible are inscribed to the child, "With
love from Santa Carla Meeting."

Children under six get a single flower. We take care to
avoid thorns and poisons; the babies tend to chew on
their flowers.

Anyway, enough – I've got to go get the supplies.
More soon, hope all's well with you.

Cheers.........................Lil

~~~~~~

No baptism or bar mitzvah

Dear Marla,

No, we don't have anything like a baptism or *bar
mitzvah*. I've always regretted that we have no formal,
or even informal, way of bringing our teens into the
adult circle. Lately, in California, they tend to drop out
of the local congregations, and to become an exclusive
"gang" at the regional gatherings. I don't know how it
is among Friends in the Yearly Meetings in other parts
of the country.

If a teen or young adult applies for membership, of course, we take their request seriously and have good "clearness" committee meetings with them. But often they don't feel drawn to apply for years, maybe until they have children of their own. Do you think this is how it is in most progressive sects?

We are working on this issue these days, in the local and regional gatherings. We are always working on one issue or another. It is an inevitable part of community life, I guess. It is hard – and also very rewarding, in terms of getting to know one another and refining our own values. Do you know what I mean?

Gotta run, more soon, be well......................Lily

~~~~~~

More on war taxes

Hi, Marla, hope all's well with you. It was actually warm here today, and I spent most of the afternoon in the garden, weeding again.

I wrote you before about paying war taxes under protest, I think. Today after Meeting for Worship, another protester and I handed out fliers to everyone suggesting that they pay under protest, too. There seemed to be some enthusiasm, which was encouraging for me personally.

We provided a sample letter that people could modify

and send to the IRS and their legislators. I guess we'll never know if they actually do it, though.

It is still balmy, and the stars are gorgeous, so I'm going to go out and sit in the dark for a while. Hope you also can get some peaceful moments of quiet on your own, dear friend.

Love.................Lily

I asked to see the sample letter for legislators and Lily sent it immediately.

SAMPLE letter for Legislators

                                        Date:_____

Legislator's <u>local</u> address

RE Paying Under Protest

Dear Congressman/Representative/etc:

I am determined to fulfill my responsibilities as a citizen of this democratic country.

Therefore, I have submitted my IRS Form 1040 and have paid my income taxes for 2010.

However, one of my responsibilities as a citizen is to let my government know that I believe it is misguided in using violence as a means of addressing international problems.

As a duty of conscience, I am opposed to the use of income tax revenue for the support of US involvement in war (or, in the Iraq and Afghanistan wars).

Therefore I am filing my IRS 1040 and paying my taxes under protest.

Please support the establishment of the proposed Peace Tax Fund, which will allow conscientious opponents of war like myself to direct their tax money into programs which support peaceful community life in the United States and around the world.

Thank you for your attention.

Sincerely yours,

Typed name and address:
_____

Copies to: _____
_____

〰〰〰〰〰〰〰〰〰〰〰〰〰〰〰〰〰〰〰〰〰〰〰〰〰

Testimonies

Dear Marla,

So glad the Quaker *Faith and Practice* got through to you finally, not too much battered. Just in time for you to look up "the Testimonies" and ask your challenging questions!

First of all, about your own faith and practice.

Quakers would say that you were "under a leading"when the idea came to you to go to Karachi to work with blind children there. We would say that you "tested the leading" with others as you slowly determined that you could afford the time, the money, the physical effort, the emotional impact, and the spiritual stretch which would be required. You went through an informal "clearness process" as you talked with your colleagues, children, friends, and even your financial manager about the idea of spending nine months in Pakistan. Quakers would have offered you a "clearness committee" to "test" whether you were really "Spirit-led" to make the trip.

Looking at the testimonies, I guess I would say that your project in Karachi responds to several of them.

- There is the testimony on equality, that all people (including blind and impoverished Pakistani children and their caregivers) have "that of God" or a divine spark within them, which should be recognized and nurtured.

- The testimony on simplicity calls for "the right ordering of our lives, placing God at the center," rather than possessions, activities, and behavior that distract us from that center. By giving up an income, you're deciding to "take no more than [your] share and to be sensitive to the needs of others."
- By working in a Muslim country, you are observing the peace testimony, "sustaining relationships of mutual human regard."
- The testimony on integrity includes this line: "When lives are centered in the Spirit, beliefs and actions are congruent." Isn't this exactly what you were saying in your letter about how the work makes you feel whole (holy?) despite the heat, the humidity, the marginal working conditions, the boring diet, and all the rest of it?

Gosh, girl, you are almost a Quaker already! Now all you need is a silent Meeting for Worship "where two or three are gathered together in [His] name." Can't you and Jeremy find two or three more Quakers to sit with? I wish I could be with you, serving and centered.....

Love...........................Lil

George Fox

Marla, it's me again. Don't rely on the *F&P* to understand our founder, George Fox. Ask Jeremy to sing you our favorite historical ditty about him, doggerel verse and all.

In my old leather britches and my shaggy, shaggy locks,
I am walking in the glory of the Light, said Fox!

Probably nowadays we'd think he was a mad man. It is told that in his heyday, Fox would walk into the middle of Church of England services and interrupt the sermon to give his own inspirational speech. When the authorities dragged him out, some of the congregants would follow and never go back again.

The bit about the "shaggy, shaggy locks" is part of the refrain. Hmmm, what are the other words? Hey, I've found them in *Rise Up Singing*.

There's a light that was shining when the world began,
There's a light that is shining in each woman and man.
There's a light that is shining in the Turk and the Jew,
And a light that is shining, friend, in me and in you.

Refrain:

Walk in the Light, wherever you may be;
Walk in the Light, wherever you may be.
In my old leather britches and my shaggy, shaggy locks,
I am walking in the glory of the Light, said Fox.

With a book and a steeple and a bell and a key,
They would bind it forever, but they can't, said he.
O the book it will perish and the steeple will fall,
But the Light will be shining at the end of it all.

    Refrain…

"If we give you a pistol, will you fight for the Lord?"
"But you can't kill the devil with a gun or a sword."
"Will you swear on the Bible?" "I will not", said he,
"For the Truth is more holy than the Book to me."

    Refrain…

There's an ocean of darkness and I drown in the night
Til I come through the darkness to the ocean of light.
You can lock me in prison but the Light will be free,
And I'll walk in the glory of the Light, said he.

    Refrain

Ask Jeremy about the tune. It'll stick in your head and you'll be humming it all day. As will I today, now that I've written about it to you!

Cheers……………………Lily

~~~~~~

Church music

Dear Marla,

Today I have basked in good old Catholic church music. I cleaned up the house this morning with the Brahms *Requiem Mass* playing in the background, and then I went this afternoon to hear a community choir do the Dvorak *Stabat Mater*. Quakers don't share the theology of these works, you know, about Jesus dying for our sins. Mostly we figure we pay for our own sins, directly or indirectly. But the music itself conveys so much better than most words I've ever encountered the human longing for forgiveness and grace. Do you know what I mean?

Do you have any western music with you? Does it seem out of place? I remember hearing Indian movie music playing loudly in the bazaars and everywhere. Have you started to get the hang of it? Isn't it weird, constantly hearing songs -- humming along, even – but not understanding any of the words because they are in Urdu/Hindi?

Wow, it is a wide, wild world we live in.

Enjoy! Lil

~~~~~~

Easter

Oh, Marla, I am glad to hear that you had a chance to attend a Christian service on Easter morning, all in the midst of that Islamic culture. I remember going to a big

Catholic Church on Christmas Eve in Karachi. It was so jammed that we could not get inside, but stood outside the open doors. And yes, the beggars were thronging all around us. They know the Christian teaching: Give to the poor.....

Here, at the Friends Meeting, as usual, we don't make a big deal of this particular holiday. The "ascension" and "resurrection" are not essential to the way most of us relate to Jesus, that fine radical teacher from Nazareth.

Because Easter egg hunts get a little grabby, there wasn't even one of those this year, at Meeting. The kids did decorate some eggs, though, and may have talked in their First Day School class about how eggs symbolize spring and new beginnings.

But I myself need some ritual and music, for Easter and some of the other holidays. So I always listen to *Jesus Christ Superstar* at Easter and put little bunny and egg decorations on my side board, with the early flowers. Kind of silly and sentimental, but fun.

More soon....................................Lil

~~~~~~

Meeting for Business

Dear Marla,

Oh, gosh, we did it today, we really can do this

consensus stuff well once in a while! Look in the *Faith and Practice* I sent you, starting on page 129. It was a tough Meeting for Business with disagreement over whether and how to renovate the First Day School rooms. (You got it that "First Day: is Sunday, right?)

Not more than about a quarter of our members attend business meeting regularly, because people think it is too foolish and boring that we can take half an hour to decide what color paint to put on the walls. What we are really doing, though, is putting our *faith* into disciplined *practice*. (By the way, the alternate name for the *Faith and Practice* is "The Discipline.")

In "meeting for worship on the occasion of business," the point is not that my color – I prefer olive green –should be chosen. The point is, can I listen to that of God in Sheila, who wants a smoky blue? She seems more agitated than the occasion merits – what's going on with her? Where is her husband today? Oh, and Janice has gone out to be with the kids; I guess the child care arrangements fell through (again). I'll ask my teenage neighbor if she would like a regular little job on Sundays. Now Harold is weighing in about the cost of paint, but Henry thinks we should not be penny-pinchers.

Well, at this point, the clerk of the Meeting (the chairperson) said something gentle and mollifying like, "Hey, good Friends, let's slow this down a little bit." He reminded us all to allow silence between speakers, to address the clerk instead of one another, to remember that our underlying task as always is to promote the well-being of our faith community. He suggested that we remember to breathe deep, and then he led us into a little time of worship.

After that, the issue was resolved within minutes. I don't even remember what colors were chosen. I know that this process has led me to know all these people better, to care about them more, and to be better able to go slow and think care-fully in all the little conflict situations that arise in my life. I <u>love</u> it that we can do this together!

Your grateful friend...............................Lily

At this point, I began to imagine creating a book out of the material Lily was sending me about Quakers. I'd edit out the remarks about our children, my work in Karachi, and so forth. Not sure how I would find a publisher, but could deal with that later. I started asking more questions about "the Religious Society of Friends," as she and Jeremy sometimes call it.

~~~~~~

Sexuality

Dear Marla,

Goodness, but you are asking all the possible questions about Quaker faith and practice, aren't you!

I don't even know how to answer your questions about sexuality. Well, at least, I don't know much about the sex lives of my fellow Quakers.

I guess I do know some basic principals we all share, though. Our core idea of the divine spark in all people means to us that all relationships, including intimate ones, must be caring and respectful. That would generally imply no involvements or intercourse with people under the age of consent, no violence or rape, no "kinky" practices except between consenting adults, no manipulation or abuse.

Our printed materials show great respect for marriage as the preferred environment for sexual intimacy, gay or straight. Adultery is definitely not OK among us. But quite a few Quaker adults are involved in sexual relationships before (and between) marriage(s).

Speaking of which, the sociologist in me has long delighted in the way that our big regional gatherings, like those of any religious denomination, serve as informal "marriage markets" where people -- people of all ages, now that divorce is so common among us – are on the look-out for likely partners among the like-minded people gathered there.

Getting even more bold, I can also confess that often on a Sunday morning in worship, I have basked in the glow of good sex the night before. It delights me even now to know that others sitting near me as we settle into the worshipful silence are perhaps remembering similar ecstasies from the night before.

We do have concerns about premature sex among young teens, though, and we make a point of organizing our teen overnight programs so that coupling is deeply discouraged. Often Friends gatherings are the only place where our teenagers are freed from intense social pressure to sexualize their friendships. At our gatherings, kids are encouraged to relate with all their peers as equal friends through conversation, work and play together. They often even sleep in the same big room, boys and girls together -- but under separate blankets and under adult supervision.

I can tell you'll be asking me next about abortion. It is an especially interesting question among Quakers, but too big to get into now. I've got to go take part in a family conference call.

Til soon.....................Lily

~~~~~~

Abortion

Dear Marla,

Good, you started on the abortion discussion with Jeremy before I could offer my two cents' worth.

I agree with him, it is a topic Quakers keep guiltily under the rug because many of us have had abortions, even though it is apparently inconsistent with our testimony that every human life is sacred. When does a human's life begin? We've never reached agreement on this question.

Virtually all of us oppose war and capitol punishment and hand guns. But many of us condone abortion when the new life might be compromised by the immaturity, poverty, or poor physical or mental health of the mother. (Some Quakers also condone "self-determination," the suicide of a person who is already terminally ill and wishes to protect his dear ones from the burdens of a slow death.)

We rarely discuss these things as a group, though. Perhaps it is because we know that we will not currently be able to reach any consensus about them. Similarly, there is no guidance offered on these matters in the <u>Faith and Practice.</u>

Once, though, years ago, I was in a gathering where some Friends talked about abortion. It was not initiated by the feminists among us. The impetus for the conversation was from a young man who was acutely grieving over an abortion his girl friend had had. It was deeply moving to hear him talk, see him weep.

Later, when I told one of my sons about it, he pointed out that many young men nowadays (and I know he includes himself) have to live their whole lives with the unresolved question of whether they might have fathered a child or two that they do not know about, perhaps a child whose life was interrupted before birth, or perhaps one that is still living somewhere. Yikes. What if some such child suddenly showed up on his doorstep?

It is 11:30 pm, my dear. Off to bed; more soon.

Cheers....................Lily

~~~~~~

Jeremy about abortion

Gosh, Marla, I almost feel as if I am in a three way conversation with you and Jeremy, the way you loop him in to these interesting conversations. I quite enjoy it.

Interesting that he missed a beat when you shared my son's remark that some men never quite know whether they have spawned an infant or not. Maybe Jeremy is gay, like you suggested, what with being single at age forty and all.

Or maybe he knows he has a child, one that he does not acknowledge or support. I once had a lover who was in that situation. I expect most Quaker men would at least support, if not publicly acknowledge.....oooh, the plot thickens.

~~~~~~

Gardening

Hi, Marla,

I am missing the Meeting attender who helped me the last two years in the task I've been working on alone this afternoon: trimming away the overgrown ivy and blackberry bushes in my back yard. I have to fight to protect the little patch of grass, about as big as a king-size bed. I always plan to lie down on that grass and watch the sky like I did as a kid, but I am afraid the neighbors will notice and think I have collapsed.

Those same neighbors worry that the ivy will harbor rats, but I've never seen one in thirteen years. I think the local cats keep them away, though the cats don't seem to scare the skunks, opossums or raccoons. Yes, right here in the middle of the city!

I am remembering the long lanky *mali* who kept up our brittle garden in Karachi all those years ago. I didn't lie on that prickly grass, either; it was used mainly for laying out the laundry to dry, as I remember. It would dry in about twenty minutes, it was so hot. Is that how laundry is done nowadays? You said you have a nice deep veranda. Does it look out over a lawn and garden?

Marla, you wrote that you'd had a bout of "Delhi belly" – par for the course, but no fun. I hope you are well over it now. I'm glad it led the managers to step up precautions in the kitchen.

Be well, my dear.

Love....................Lily

~~~~~~

Centering down

So now, Marla, to try to answer your good questions about "centering down" in Meeting for Worship – or at any other time, for that matter.

Yes, I would say this is like all kinds of meditation. You know: find an uninterrupted space, a conducive position, quiet your body, still your thoughts. There is always "the monkey mind" to deal with, the internal chitter-chatter. So over and over, you just gently go back to the stillness, if you can.

Some Quakers talk about "waiting worship" and having an expectant attitude. They expect to "hear the still, small voice of God." Others are less sure about God, or God having a voice, but they know that new and wise ideas may arise from deep within a still mind. It is an amazing thing that happens – especially when someone else speaks from the silence and says exactly the words you need to hear, or perhaps were about to say.

From time to time, we talk together about our practices, and many of us read inspiring guides to meditation written by Quakers or others, especially Buddhists. We often borrow from these others -- following the breath, progressive relaxation, internally chanting a mantra (*Omm, Be Here Now*), counting backwards from ten to one, anything that works.

For some verbal people like me, the hyperactive intellect is a problem in worship. I wonder wistfully what it would be like to be a cool, calm person with a less verbal relationship to the world. Sometimes handwork like sewing or knitting can slow me down, especially when the day's work is done. A candle-lit "altar" to look at helps, too.

But we don't have these helps in Meeting for Worship at eleven o'clock on Sunday morning. Even in the silence, there can be distractions, especially if you know a lot about the people and their problems, if someone's absence causes you concern, if a sniffle across the room makes you look up to see if someone is crying.

So the disciplines of meditation are useful. Sometimes what works for me is to try to be "invisible." Like playing hide and seek when you're little. You know that if you don't move and barely breathe, you can almost make yourself disappear. It's a terrific feeling, not holding on to any self or ego for a few moments, even though you are wide awake.

Hey, by the way, a weird story. One time years ago, in the middle of a busy day, at my desk at work, with my back to the door, I tried getting invisible, just to take a break. For about five minutes, maybe. Just after I stopped, breathed deep and went back to my paperwork, a colleague popped in and said, "Oh, you're here! I came by just a minute ago and I didn't see you here." I was kind of spooked!

Well, this has become a long letter and I haven't told the ordinary news. But it'll wait.

Be well, good friend.

Lily

I kept pushing new questions about Quakers, but I didn't tell Lillian my notion about a book. She cheerfully answered me, even when it was a little hard – as in talking about divorce.

Divorce

Dear Marla,

Yes, Jeremy is right, the truth is we Quakers are as likely to divorce as anyone else nowadays. I am always sorry about it, and I am sorry to hear that his parents are not together any longer. At least they lasted through the child-rearing years, I gather? What siblings does Jeremy have, if any?

I was shocked the first time I met a Quaker who was divorced, it was so rare. But that was about forty years ago. Forty years is a long span in the socially revolutionary times you and I have lived through!

This topic still makes me uneasy, thirty years after my own divorce.

Using the traditional Quaker marriage vows, I promised, "in the presence of God and these our friends, to be unto thee a loving and faithful wife so long as we both shall live."

I rationalize that I did remain loving and faithful. The *loving* thing to do at the time we separated, the way to respond *faithfully* to the needs of my husband (and the safety of our children) was to release him from the marriage.

I know you are going to want to know more, and I will tell it, but not in this letter.

Yes, I will tell it right now. My husband was yearning after young men with such fervor that I felt his frustration was putting our very lives in danger. He would get crazy with rage sometimes. So I let him go.

People in Meeting helped us figure out the separation. They held him in the Light just the same as they held me and the children. They have always held us. They stood by us during the wild teenage years of my half-black daughter. They supported us through the mental illness of my eldest son.

The thing is that Quakers look for that of God in every person, gay or straight, black or white, more or less coherent, more or less crazy. The divine spark is always there to be nurtured.

Your lucky, loving friend..........................*Lily*

Well, that was a letter fraught with history. I asked more, and I answered as best I could Lily's questions about Jeremy's family. He was opening up to me more and more.

~~~~~~

Quaker families

Dear Marla,

Just a quickie to say that I got your letter saying that Jeremy has a younger sister, that his mother is no longer part of their local Meeting, and that he feels closer to his father than to other members of his family.

Don't worry about me. My resilient children are doing well, and mainly I feel blessed.

It is an advantage to me to be familiar with traits that tend to scare other people. Gay, black, mentally ill, high school drop-out, poor, angry, violent, alcoholic, compulsive – these are not "those people" to me, they are my own family. I know and love them. I have learned a lot about how I can live with them.

More than that, we have been embraced by my faith community during the hard years. My family and I have been encouraged and supported us as we got our bearings and learned to thrive in the larger society. We are lucky!

More another time………………..Lil

~~~~~~

Children's Day

Dear Marla,

Remember I mentioned a while back that I was starting on the preparations for the annual Children's Day celebration at Meeting? Well, we had it today. It took 31 minutes! It was totally wonderful.

One of the babies did chew on her flower, as we had anticipated. There was one disaster – a new six year old dropped his gift, the framed plaque reading *Let us then try what love can do* (William Penn), and it cracked. But I have extra frames and can replace it next Sunday. Next year we'll go back to the plastic frames!

We always have a reading from <u>The Prophet</u>, that wonderful one about children which starts,

> *Your children are not your children. They are the sons and daughters of Life's longing for itself. They come through you but not from you, and though they are with you yet they belong not to you.*

As the event planner, my concern is always that a healthy number of adults who are not parents show up, as a gesture of support for the parents. I try to recruit several of them for specific roles. Today there were eleven non-parents (and fifteen parents), and I was satisfied.

We finished up with a rollicking rendition of *This Little Light of Mine* with three guitars (non-parents) accompanying. I am so fond of these people!

Am I writing too much about my Friends Meeting? It comes partly from writing to you mostly on Sunday evenings, when I have just come from there.

I do want to respond soon to your remarks about the challenges you are working with on the job. But, golly, dolly, I am worn out, so I'll put it off until later this week.

Love.....................Lillian

Lillian did sympathize with my work situation – power outages, water shortage, one difficult program aide, and once a bomb scare as fighter planes went overhead. But meanwhile, Jeremy told me his father was a production editor who helped authors create books and I began to wonder if he could help produce the Quaker book I was imagining. I still didn't tell Lily about it.

~~~~~~

Quaker gatherings

Dear Marla,

Goodness, I've just come home from a Quarterly Meeting weekend; in June I am to go to a family work camp (taking my non-Quaker offspring); and now I must register for the Friends General Conference (FGC) Gathering coming up in July. After that, there will be

Yearly Meeting. Am I becoming a Quaker junkie? Help! Most Friends do not attend a fraction of these gatherings.

But still. I have been hearing about the FGC Gathering for years, but have never been able to attend before. At this nation-wide gathering (it'll be near Pittsburg this year), no tedious business is transacted. Instead, there are close to three dozen five-day workshops, scores of interest groups, and many entertainments. There is lots of worship, much chatting over meals, beautiful places to walk, a huge bookstore, and so forth.

So going there is a special treat. It will be made even better by the fact that my sister from upstate New York is going to come and share a room with me. And I am going to come home across the country by train!

Anyway, more about all this later. Meanwhile, tell more about your new program aide.

Cheers.....................Lil

~~~~~~~~~~~~~~~~~~~~~~~~~~~~~~~~~~~~~~~

Faith community

Well, Marla, to answer your question, I was raised in a Quaker family, but out of my three siblings, only the sister I will meet in Pittsburg is still a Quaker. And none of my kids is currently a member of a Friends Meeting. It is a long story, but it is not at all unusual in the Quaker community.

Among my siblings and children, some are still spiritual seekers. But one has become a cynical atheist. One is married to a non-believer who likes her to be home on Sunday mornings. One has become a Muslim, and one has become a fundamentalist. And so on. We were taught to be seekers, and you never know what we will find!

My own feeling is that it is very desirable in this tough world to belong to a close community, no matter what you believe. In urban America, the most likely option is a church-based community, don't you think? It is worth the inevitable little struggles to maintain ones participation in the community, it seems to me. Especially if you're single – and we are almost all at risk of becoming single, if we are not already.

Fortunately, among Friends, a person's theology can shift quite a lot over the decades and still fit within the range the Quaker community finds acceptable.

I don't care so much, about some of my dear ones, that they are not Quakers. I do worry when they are not part of a close community where they feel they belong. I guess they feel close to people at work, or in a neighborhood, but these can be minimal connections and are always changing. And American families are so spread out geographically, and so often broken or somehow dysfunctional.

I know you have moved in and out of various churches, and for good reason. I'm glad for you that, right now, you are living in a close-knit community – though it may be too close in some ways, as you have said. Still, I hope that you will find a good church to belong to when you return to the US,

Well, one step at a time.*

Cheers……………………..Lillian

*Yes, I know that phrase comes from AA and that Alcoholics Anonymous serves that communal role to a certain extent, too. I am glad for people who belong.

~~~~~~

Quaker work camp

Dear Marla,

I came back from the family work camp and found two letters from you, and then another came today. Riches! It will take me a while to catch up.

My daughter Lauren brought her 8 year old out and visited for a wonderful couple of days. Then Lauren went back to Colorado, and Lina and I piled in with the boy cousins (age 15, 8 and 5), left the cool Bay Area, and went off to the Quaker work camp in the Sierras.

It was 105 degrees the first day! But it is a beautiful setting of fields and woods, rolling hills and rustic cabins.

The program was to include hard physical labor, for all ages from five on up, for half the day, then swimming and singing and goofing off. There were about thirty five of us all told, and the oldest participant this year was just over seventy.

The work included painting, weeding, chopping trees and branches, clearing out the grey water channel, replacing the drapes in the main house, taking lots of accumulated stuff to the dump.

The "playing" (if you were an energetic kid) included much running on the gorgeous green soccer field. In the late afternoons, there was more "easy" work: helping the cook to prep supper, then after supper cleaning the dining room, running the dishwasher, and washing all the pots and pans. I did get tired.

Beforehand, people kept asking me what kind of a vacation this would be. "Only Quakers would think it fun to spend a week like that," my neighbor said, shaking her head in disbelief.

It *was* dreadfully hot. Walking up and down the hill to our rustic little cottage *was* hard on my arthritic feet. And I really *don't* like vegetarian food.

But this is the only Quaker venue I know of where, year after year, people of all ages really spend time and share everything *together*. Including, most notably, the teens. The teenage kids with us during this work week were great with elders and little kids, both. We all learned new skills and developed new muscle (and blisters). While we were at it, we adults (and the teens, too) displayed attitudes and values that we think are important for the little kids to learn: willingness to work hard, get dirty, be patient, share with others, learn, help......

Yes, you got it – this is my main chance during the year to subtly indoctrinate my grandchildren in Quaker values. And not so subtly when it comes to the books I bring for them to read before bed. And you know what, they sit easily in a half hour worship every day, too, soaking up that special silence. There's no way I can explain it, they just get to experience it.

There's more to tell, and you've asked questions. But I'll have to put off the rest until I slog through all these bills and e-mails. How can so much accumulate in only one week!

Keep well..........................Lily

~~~~~~

Friends General Conference gathering plans

I'm barely home from work camp and now I'm getting ready to go to the FGC Gathering in Pennsylvania. It's kind of expensive for me, especially when you add in travel costs, but this is my once-in-a-lifetime chance, and my sister will meet me there. And there will be a workshop I really need to attend.

I've told you about not being a conventional Christian. But I haven't confessed before that I have been struggling painfully the last seven or eight years with the slow erosion of my faith in any kind of God. It is hard to talk about it.

For decades, I had a mystical sense of Presence. All the major life-changing decisions in my life I have experienced as "leadings," as we call them, a kind of divine call. Then I began to lose this faith. I think it was around the time my revered father died.

I remember a friend telling me, in a skuzzy little diner on the way to Muir Woods, that I would not be hit by lightning if I did not believe in a personal God. She was/is a Buddhist. It had a big impact on me. Not because I believed in the lightning, but because I needed this kind of reassurance from someone I respected.

Then my crusty old Jungian friend kept me moving along the same path, not that I really wanted to go there. Slowly I lost my mystical faith and became an unhappy and wistful post-theist. I have been in this condition quite a while now.

At the FGC Gathering, a person can spend a whole week talking with others about any one subject. I've signed up for one of the workshops on non-theism.

Wish me luck.

How we say that in Quakerese is, "Hold me in the Light."

Love.......................Lily

~~~~~~

Post-theism

Well, as expected, I spent the whole week at the FGC gathering immersed in questions about the existence of God.

It is a relatively new area of exploration among Quakers, though the British are ahead of us Americans. By devoting solid time to coherent thinking and discussion with other serious Friends, I was able to get much clearer and more confidant about my current beliefs.

Of course, I am deeply grounded in the Christian ethical system, but we Quakers also characterize ourselves as seekers. Like many of us, I have been a student of other faith systems at the same time that I participate in Quaker worship and business. I have read so much. And I have worshipped with Catholics and Buddhists often.

Many Quakers and other seekers call the divine by names other than God. But I've noticed that even when people, including myself, speak of "the Spirit," there is still often an anthropomorphic cast to it, a vague image of a wise entity able to speak to us and guide our decisions.

What if there is no such guide? What if it is just a human projection? These are big questions, almost too scary to contemplate. But these were the topics discussed at the workshop I attended. It seemed safe in this group of Quakers from all over the country, with a facilitator from Great Britain.

Without belief in any kind of God, we agreed, reverence and awe can remain our stance towards life. A non-theist can still be a follower of Jesus of Nazareth, that radical, independent thinker who introduced us to the idea that the divine spirit is inherent in every person.

My workshop focused on how theists and non-theists, like Christocentrics and post-Christians, can worship and work together in Friends Meetings without clashing. It really is the great genius of Quakerism, that your faith and theology can waiver, grow, and change without your having to leave your faith community.

Who said "God is too big to put in a box"? It wasn't one of us, but we believe it. There is almost no dogma in Quakerism. We expect "continuing revelation" and the emergence of new truths. The only absolute for us is that "there is that of God in every person," a divine spark which we are to seek, nurture, and never extinguish (by disrespect, abuse, violence or killing).

Well, this is a huge topic and I feel a little garbled, just touching on it like this. See what Jeremy says, if you get a chance to talk with him about it.

Cheers.....................Lillian

~~~~~~

Wistful post theist

Thanks for picking up on my little phrase, "wistful post-theist" a couple of letters back, Marla. You really are a fine correspondent with whom to share these meaty religious ideas.

There are several kinds of non-theist, we agreed at the Gathering. An atheist as one who was never taken to church or Sunday School as a child and never learned any concepts of God or Christ; or did learn the stories but, being of a scientific bent, rejected it all during his (or sometimes her) college years.

That does not describe me. Post-theist seems a better descriptive for me. Surely, having long been a believing mystic who was constantly aware of the divine presence, my experience has been very different from that of the ordinary atheist. Having unwillingly lost my faith, I am in a very different condition from one who never in his adult years had any faith in the first place.

For years after this change came upon me, I felt totally bereft – and I still am wistful. It was so lovely having access to that sense of peace and guidance whenever I turned expectantly in that direction!

For a long time, I kept hoping it was just that "dark night of the soul" people speak of so often. But it has not been a passing phenomenon. Slowly I found books to read* which let me know I was not alone. Slowly, hinting to other Quakers about my new state of mind, I began to trust that I would not be rejected because I had, through no intention of my own, lost my old faith. David Boulton's collection of Quaker essays, *Godless for God's Sake*, and the FGC Gathering sessions were especially helpful for me.

Meanwhile, through it all – eight to ten years – I have been sustained by my habitual practices as a Friend trying to live up to the Quaker Testimonies. Thank goodness! For me, the title of our guide book, <u>Faith and Practice</u>, could almost be *faith and/or practice!*

Not that one has to be a Quaker to pursue these same values – you are doing it yourself, especially during this year of service to blind children in Pakistan. Thanks, by the way – your description of little Ameen was especially vibrant. You should write a book – or perhaps your letters to me and others during this year can be shaped into a book, what do you think? Of course I am keeping all that come to me. Will your other correspondents be saving theirs? Do you have copies?

Your description of all the scrawny yellow "pi dogs" worries me. In my day, they were believed often to be rabid. Remember that incredible description in one of Rumer Godden's books about the child who got bitten and had to go through the series of shots in the stomach? Please be careful!

Your ever-loving, blue-eyed friend...............Lillian

*You'll want to know titles and authors, won't you! Let's see: *Why God Won't Go Away,* by Andrew Newberg et al; *Meeting Jesus Again for the First Time*, by Marcus Borg; *Why I am not a Christian*, by Bertrand Russell, *History of God*, by Karen Armstrong; *Godless Morality*, by Richard Holloway. And others.

I suppose all the Jungian and Buddhist stuff I read in my forties also had an effect. Have you explored this way, too?

~~~~~~

Limerick

Hey, Marla,

Get this! Speaking of "wrestling with God," with belief vs non-belief, a friend in Meeting today told me a wonderful limerick he'd heard. It sounds like Ogden Nash but isn't.

Yesterday upon the stair
I met a man who wasn't there.
He wasn't there again today.
I sure do wish he'd go away!

This really is how I feel about God a lot of the time!

Cheers…………………..Lily

~~~~~~

Deep worship

Oh, Marla, it seemed to me that our Meeting for Worship was deeply "gathered" today. Sometimes we call it "covered" – doesn't that suggest angel wings over us all?! A gathered Meeting is one where you sense that almost everyone present is focused in the same direction, sharing the same intention. Often it happens after spoken ministry that is moving to us all, but sometimes, like today, it is at a deeper level than that. It is hard to describe. It doesn't happen very often, but it is what we are all yearning for, the sense of being truly together in the Divine Presence.

By the way, I am noticing that doubting the existence of any kind of Divinity other than some sort of Holy Spirit did not prevent me from having this experience. Phew, what a relief! I guess there are still depths to my soul, however my rational mind is interpreting the world.

Your lucky friend…………………Lily

Language, Bible

Dear good friend and spiritual companion,

You are right that when I hear Christ-centered Friends speak in Worship, and when I play the old hymns, I hear words that I have to translate to make them fit my new theology. Or non-theology. But as we agreed at the FGC Gathering, translation is needed only when I am thinking about what my own words will be. When I am just listening with love to others, I know what their words mean to them, and there is no need to translate.

The harder thing for me is that I have lost the use of this language myself. I can no longer speak easily of God or guidance or The Comforter.

Hardest of all is not being able just now to speak with confidence about "leadings." All the major decisions of my life have arisen from what I experienced at the time as divine leadings. It is a loss (even if more accurate) to think of these now as having simply been the best impulses of my own deepest consciousness.

There are vital parts of the traditional Quaker language which still work well for me, however. They include love, commitment, community, simplicity, integrity and so on. All the Quaker testimonies, and all the advices and queries still apply fully to my life.

The Bible (per your question) is not more important to me personally than the many other inspired religious writings of human history, many of which I have read. But many other Friends study the Bible, alone and together. Generally they "understand the Bible as a record arising from similar struggles to comprehend God's ways with people," as it says in the <u>Faith and Practice,</u> *p 83.*

> *The same Spirit which inspired the writers of the Bible is the Spirit which gives us understanding of it: it is this which is important to us rather than the literal words of scripture. Hence, while quotations from the Bible may illuminate a truth for us, we would not use them to prove a truth.*

Dear friend, what an unexpected opportunity you are providing for this exchange. I hope your daily life there is going well, as mine is here.

Re daily life, my fifteen-year old grandson is visiting me weekly while he is in town for the summer with his father, and I am intrigued and pleased to find him quite interested in religious matters. No big theological discussions, but he wants to visit churches, wear a crucifix, attend Catholic events with his paternal family, etc. Although he is currently pursuing quite a different religious tradition than mine, it is still an affirmation for me, to whom religious commitment is so crucial. My own children, I guess I've said before, are not so inclined, at least not just now.

Be well, send news, say hi to Jeremy for me.

Cheers……………………….Lily

Well, she hooked me with that letter and I wrote back quite a little essay about how one could use transactional analysis to think about people's religious beliefs. Not that Eric Berne got into that topic in I'm OK, You're OK. I won't here, either – Lillian translated it pretty well in her next letter.

~~~~~~

Transactional Analysis and religious practice

Oh, Marla, I was so interested in your use of transactional analysis to explain how belief in a God or Guide or Comforter works to shift the believer out of a "not-OK child" mode.

I understand the idea that anything which relieves the level of anxiety will enable a person to think more clearly about the problem at hand. Invoking the sense of divine guidance (aka praying) will in fact relieve anxiety. It will almost always help a believer to shift away from fear or need to a sense of confidence. Saves people from despair and damage! So you could say that there is an evolutionary advantage to being a believer, huh?

I guess the psychology of meditation, of any kind of

sitting in silence, works in the same way. When I sit still for a while, and breathe deep, I calm down from whatever was bothering me. After a while, my grasping ego begins to fade out, and my perceptions clear. Is it really that simple?

It doesn't make my life less busy, though! Gotta run............... Lily

I got to talking to Jeremy about all this, too, and about the bigger regional Quaker gatherings Lillian was telling me about. He commented that people also attend these meetings on the look-out, conscious or not, for potential partners. So I asked Lily about that.

~~~~~~

Non-romantic radical

Goodness, no, Marla, there's no one at Yearly Meeting of romantic interest to me. I don't do romantic any more, remember? The cost always exceeds the benefit nowadays, given my age and general level of independence. What would I need a man for?

Well, I admit I would like more chance at deep discussions with straight men, even though I tend to expect arrogance from them. I am on the look out for a sense of superiority even from Quaker men, who are probably better than most in this regard. So I put myself in a double bind, don't I?

(One tall, blue-eyed man once pointed out to me that, being tall and blue-eyed myself, I have a similar advantage in society to his. I project the same confidence he does, confidence that is sometimes seen as arrogance by others. Ack!)

I don't have the same negativity about non-professional men, dark-skinned men, gay men, or poor men. I was never a women's libber, but I picked up the prejudices of my time, I guess. Shucks.

Speaking if which, how is Jeremy doing these days? And what about the American family from Syracuse? I love hearing about your work, but also want to be reassured that you have good supportive friends from your home land.

I've got to stop now to go down town and join a protest rally against an insidious video game called *America's Army*. It was developed by contractors for the US Army and can be downloaded for free from the Internet. It is a military recruitment tool targeting young kids in defiance of an international convention signed by the US that children under seventeen will not be recruited. I am going to help put flyers on parked cars.

So bye for now!

Your radical friend..........................Lillian

~~~~~~

Racism theme

Dear Marla,

Do you mind if I go on a bit more about Yearly
Meeting? I am still under its spell, even though I was
only there half the time.

Every year there seems to be some central issue which
rises to the surface for our consideration, and this year
it was racism and white privilege. Quaker history in
this regard is not much better than any other, and
modern day Quakers, both white and black, still
struggle to be aware of their own blind spots and
prejudices.

However, this concern does not "speak to my
condition," as we say. I know I am guilty of making
some assumptions from a position of privilege and
confidence, but I believe I am not racist.

You have to be taught racism, you are not born with it.
By chance, I was never taught it, quite the opposite.
My daughter is half black, her husband is African, their
child and a third of my nieces and nephews are part
black. I have deliberately chosen to work for twenty
years in a deeply integrated organization. My long-

83

time lover was African. I hate even to point all this out -- I never even think about skin color. It makes me angry to be classed among racists. Does my defensiveness indicate that somehow I actually am?

Perhaps I get defensive because I am a victim of prejudice, too. No one looking at me when I am away from my work and family can guess that my life is so entwined with people of other races.

It especially bothered me during this challenging Yearly Meeting session because there was no acknowledgement of the anti-racist history of Pacific Yearly Meeting itself. It was in this group, forty years ago, that slightly older Quaker couples modeled for my husband and me the possibility of integrating our family by adopting children of skin color other than our own. Lots of us who were at that gathering last week have racially integrated histories, families, and work places like mine.

But many people assume from the white and middle-class way we *look* that we have no such experience. (A white man stood jiggling a black baby at the side of the room during the most heated discussion on this topic, and I wished it were thirty five years ago, when I was the white parent holding my own African-American baby at the edge of the same gathering.)

I feel that what Quakers really need to address at this point in history is prejudice about class and political party. The people about whom we make unkind assumptions these days are not people with dark skin, but people with little education, people who attend fundamentalist churches, and people who vote Republican. We often avoid these people as we once avoided African Americans. We say totally irresponsible things about them, and most of us do not go out of our way to get to know them. Well, Republican relatives are an exception, perhaps, if we have them. But even then, we often "agree to disagree" and fail to find gentle ways to discuss the hard topics with them.

Maybe I should write something about this for the *Friends Journal* or the *Western Friend*. Surely I should stop ranting about it now, when really I should be correcting my own negative stereotype about the tall, handsome, blue-eyed men of this world.

No one ever said it would be easy to lead a closely examined life. I'll rest up now by doing the dishes and the laundry. It is a bleak and cold summer day, always depressing. Maybe some good music will cheer me up. Do you know about Pandora radio, streaming and free over the Internet? Wonderful!

Cheers to you, too, good friend.........................Lily

Well, that was an interesting letter! I didn't know all that before. I asked about the lover, and she answered promptly. I wonder if she'll be willing to publish all this, if the book project works out.

Full service friends

Well, Marla, truth to tell, most of my Quaker associates didn't know anything about my personal life after my divorce. They wouldn't have minded that my long time lover was an African, but they might have minded that he and I always knew we would never live together. Our temperaments and our values were not compatible enough for that. And neither of us felt a need for daily companionship and support.

Ironic, isn't it? When you and I were twenty, "living together" without marriage was deeply objectionable to our parents. By the time we were forty, living together was socially acceptable, but some were still dubious about the idea of "full-service" friendships without cohabitation or movement in that direction.

The thing that worked so well for Jake and me those twelve years was that, being so independent, and burdening one another so little with our needs and hopes and delusions, we were able to see one another with a wonderful clarity and maturity, I think.

But then, all of us gain clarity and maturity with the years. Thank goodness!

Cheers.....................Lily

Knitting for baby

Hey, hi, once again, dear Marla,

Tell me if I am getting ahead of myself and bringing down bad luck...I have started eagerly knitting a blanket for a baby who may not even be conceived yet!

It's partly just that I get restless in Meeting for Business, which goes at a slow and deliberate pace, unless I can discharge energy and attention into some kind of handwork. So often I knit, and today I was ready to start on something new.

I also very much want to support the baby project undertaken by my friend, Caroline, all on her own. Did I mention it before? Caroline is a single, vivacious, thirty five year old Lesbian in Westin Meeting. She has thoughtfully and carefully "reached clearness" about trying to get pregnant, even though she has neither a male nor a female partner. She is pursuing artificial insemination ("insem," she calls it), and it is as nerve-wracking as for any young wife trying to get pregnant, with the great rush of disappointment when her period comes again.

I admit that it is irrational and inconsistent of me to be so enthusiastic about Caroline's plan, when I am so concerned about over-population of the planet that I adopted two of my own children rather than produce new ones. Help! On some level, I think it wrong to have a baby just to satisfy a personal need. But the instinct is enormously strong. I'd have gone to any lengths to have a baby myself. What do you think?

Caroline has not told many in her Meeting about this project yet, but if she does conceive, of course it will become evident. I have not heard of any similar solo pregnancy among Quakers anywhere, and I don't know how people will respond. In many of the bigger California Meetings, we have male couples and single gay people with adopted children, and female couples with born children. But no birth to a single gay woman via "insem" that I know of.

As I write this to you, I realize that I am moving towards making a commitment to support Caroline in this, in whatever ways seem needed. Even though it is inconsistent with my own decisions in the past. So now I am the one seeking clearness!

I guess I had better talk to her more about this, huh.

Tell me what you think and then stay tuned!

Your confused buddy...........................Lil

Good gracious, I got talking to Jeremy about this insem idea, and suddenly he was confiding in me in a way I never remotely expected. I wrote to Lillian in a whirlwind!

Transman

Oh my gosh, Marla, my head is spinning, just like yours. Jeremy is a transman!

No, I don't mind that you told Jeremy about the Caroline pregnancy project, seeking his perspective and response.

But who would have guessed that his Meeting has handled something even bigger, his own transition from female to male. They are not even in liberal California!

Yes, we have had experience with this process in our Meeting.

Yes, we have full-fledged members who are transsexual.

Yes, it is sometimes quite successful and sometimes not, depending substantially on the bone structure, vocal cords, and physical make up of the transitioning person.

Yes, there are good things to read, especially Jamison Green's *Becoming a Visible Man,* which I can send you if Jeremy doesn't have it for you to borrow.

The thing is, our Meeting, like Jeremy's, was told in

advance of the change a Friend was planning. There may even have been a clearness committee to help her/him decide. And then we watched and tracked the changes as they came along.

You have had much more of a shock, having it suddenly revealed that your perception of someone was off the mark in such an important way. You'll be thinking you can't believe your own eyes any more.

But Jamison Green would say your perceptions were fine, that it was Jeremy's original incarnation that was wrong. Green tells that when he first came out, to a macho men's group he belonged to, he told them that *there was once a little boy named Jamie* who found himself in the wrong body, a girl's body, and therefore in the wrong life. He suffered in many ways for many years until he could bring his body into conformity with his true self.

It's not like there was once a little girl who changed to become a boy. He knew himself to be a little boy from the beginning.

The good news is that if you are totally shocked, it means Jeremy's transition has been really successful.

Write back right away – your head must be whirling.

Cheers………………..Lily

More about Jeremy

Dear Marla,

Emerging from sleep has always been a slow process for me – I come wavering up as if from deep water.

But this morning as I approached the surface, I suddenly remembered your big news yesterday and I bobbed up fast!

Are you still feeling "duped"? I know I get a silly feeling of resentment when I cannot determine the gender identity of people on the bus. It is so deeply ingrained in us to first and foremost identify every person by gender that we don't like it when we cannot. Think of it, though – children at age two don't classify people as male or female. They just accept us as whole. Holy.

Anyway, I suppose by now Jeremy himself has helped you to shift your mind set about him. He's still the good friend and co-worker he was before, right? It's just that now you also know what great strength of character he has had, to recognize his own "gender dysphoria" and go through all the long, painful and expensive process of making the transition. Wish I could meet the guy!

Love.......................Lily

~~~~~~

Gender changes

Dear Marla,

No, I do not in the least think you are an old fogy or a
prude because you are in a whirl still about Jeremy. Of
course you cannot help wondering about the
technicalities of love-making when a person's genitalia
have been surgically altered.

I myself assume that hands and mouth come more into
play, perhaps, than with conventionally sexed people.
Not always a bad thing, right?

This was a big preoccupation of mine when I first
talked with a woman whose husband of several years
was becoming a woman. Would it all be OK for the
wife, in bed, I mean? And of course now, partnered
with another woman, she would often be seen as a
Lesbian, which was not how she perceived herself.

Her response was wonderful. She said that her partner
of so many years had been miserable all the time and
now had a chance at happiness. How could she stand
in the way of that?

I am sobered to think, though, about the cultural milieu
of Karachi, and to realize the burden of discretion
Jeremy has put on you with his confession. I remember
how prominent the tall flamboyant cross-dressers

always are at Muslim celebrations there, but I am not at all sure that means that trans-gender surgery etc would be accepted. It is a good thing Jeremy's tour of duty is coming to an end soon, I guess. Do you think perhaps we shouldn't write too much more about it?

Still, congratulations that Jeremy saw in you a confidant who could be trusted. How hard it must have been for him to hold his secret totally alone for most of a year. Now that he has shared this intimate information with you, you will miss him even more when he goes.

In answer to your last question, with our only real doctrine being that "there is that of God in every person," Quakers are generally pretty accepting of everyone, old or young, gay or straight, fat or thin, black or white, etc. But I know that many of the Establishment churches are also more and more welcoming, and I have the impression that many of the new coffee-house congregations are open-hearted towards those with unconventional sexual orientations. So I don't think Quakers are too special in this regard.

I love how you refer me to the Virgin Mary and say that, like her, we are to "take all these things and ponder them in [our] hearts."

Be well, keep up the good work.

Love…………………….Lil

So now Jeremy and I were talking together about how Muslims might react if they knew his secret identity. We worried about discussing it on line. Eager to think the best of the culture around me, pretty conservative about personal behaviors, I glommed onto a hopeful passage about Islam and World Peace, and sent it to Lil, even though it didn't say anything about "alternative" sexual orientations.

Islam and World Peace

"The qualities of Allah that exist within the heart of one with determined faith must reach out, enter the heart of another, and give him comfort and peace...This is how true Islam spreads, not by going to war to conquer other lands."

(M.R. Bawa Muhaiyaddeen, from " Islam and World Peace – Explanations of a Sufi" pps. 92-93)

***

In the current period of history, it would be easy for someone who is unfamiliar with the teachings of Islam to conclude -- from a casual reading of the headlines – that Islam is a religion of war and terror. But this is not the case.

The most basic concept in Islam is the concept of surrender to Allah with absolute faith. Indeed, one can become a Muslim simply by declaring one's faith in

Allah and his Messenger, the prophet Muhammad.

This declaration of faith in God and his prophet Muhammad is the first pillar (or most basic foundation) of Islam. There are four other pillars. They include prayer, charity, fasting and pilgrimage. All of them are oriented toward creating an inner sensitivity toward the needs of others and building an awareness of our spiritual unity with others.

- Prayer – five times daily – this prayer or *salat* is thought of as being an inner fight against bad qualities like anger, vengeance, lust and so forth.
- Charity – is put forth as a way of cultivating an awareness of the needs of others and the responsibility we have as members of one family to care for each other.
- Fasting – is undertaken as a way of voluntarily exposing oneself to the pain of hunger
- experienced by others.
- Pilgrimage – the spiritual content of the pilgrimage is for a person to "die before death" or to become dead to worldly things and focus instead on spiritual qualities.

Thus, the five pillars of Islam are all concerned with cultivating the kind of awareness of oneself and of others that will transform a person into a person of peace. There is nothing in these five pillars that supports the idea of warring against other people at any time, or for any reason.

While the holy book of Islam, the Quran, does discuss

matters pertaining to war, it does so in the spirit of the Prophet Muhammad trying to tone down the excesses of wars of his time. A major purpose of the sections of the Quran that discuss warfare seems to be to limit the pursuit of war to certain clearly defined just-war circumstances and to establish certain just rules for one's comportment in warfare.

Thus, the case is made by Bawa Muhaiyaddeen that the underlying purpose of the Quran in this regard is to move people away from the pursuit of warfare and toward the recognition of their unity and community with all other human beings.

Rick Boardman – July 2007

~~~~~~
....

Islam

Oooh, this feels especially high tech, getting an attachment to an e-mail from Pakistan.

Jeremy was right, this is a very nice statement about the Islamic desire for peace.

I guess other Muslims at other times may have more assertive attitudes towards the world, but this is certainly the one we should be spreading around these days, to counter the hostile views of *jihad* and Islamic fundamentalism and so forth. I will send it on to my various lists.

It is sweet of Jeremy to appreciate my letters, when you share them, and to accept my being in the loop about his own story. I am still holding him in my heart these days.

It is certainly prudent for you to hear his views as well as mine on Quaker faith and practice, as none of us are reliable to tell the whole story! I bet Jeremy likes to talk Quakerism because it offsets that little residual homesickness everyone feels when they live in a foreign land. How much longer will he be staying?

Yours.............................Lil

~~~~~~

Jewish conversion

All right, here's a new one, good friend, now that we are into ecumenicalism. (Ecumenism?)

My friend Lynette, a long-time observing Episcopalian, is converting to Judaism!

I don't know the whole story yet. But I know that she has been studying Torah for years, while diligently attending the Episcopal Church, though getting more and more doubtful about Episcopalian theological creeds.

Apparently reform Jews are more liberal about gay

clergy and gay marriage than Episcopalians. Apparently reform Jews expect and accept the idea that ones understanding of the nature of God is going to change over the course of the years. Sounds like the open-mindedness we Quakers are struggling to attain! Lynette really likes that.

I am very proud of her for working through this whole process and taking this big step. She will be officially inducted/welcomed/blessed by her synagogue on a Sabbath soon, and I am going to go out of my way to be there. Probably many of us in our fifties and sixties are working hard on questions of religious identity. But mostly we don't talk about it and people don't know we are doing it. So I am for raising a loud hurrah for Lynnette!

She told me that lots of older Jewish women who came of age (thirteen or so) before *bat mitzvahs* were available to girls are celebrating them now. One woman in her congregation recently had her *bat mitzvah* on the day before her hundredth birthday.

I am jealous! There is so much more experience and depth to our faith as we get old that this is the time, it seems to me, to renew, revise, declare and celebrate. Instead, mostly, in whatever denomination we belong to, we just plod along in the old ruts, doing the work of the congregation, following the rituals, hearing the same old stories.

Or maybe it is always a zigzag course between the times of plodding and the times of renewing. I'm ready for renewal!

Meanwhile, at least there are always new versions of the same old irritations and issues in my faith community.

Cheers............................Lil

~~~~~~

Buddhism

Dear Marla,

Thanks for suggesting the Wayne Dosick book as a resource for understanding Judaism. In the library here, it is maintained as a reference book and you can't take it out. I sat on the floor in the stacks and read a bit, and I may try to get it second-hand from Amazon.

Regarding your comments on Buddhism as also being very permissive about ones concept of God, I thought that the more anthropomorphic ideas about the Divine were not much tolerated in their circles.

It is certainly true, though, that Quakers at the far left end of the theological continuum tend to be attracted to Buddhism. My British Quaker friend, Jim Pym, wrote a good book about the overlap. It's called *You Don't Have to Sit on the Floor*. Great title, huh?

In fact, it was when Jim and his wife first visited me here and went looking for the local *zendo* that I started "sitting zazen" there. Because of my joints, I can't sit on the floor, but they have a few chairs.

In Meeting, we sit in a circle facing in. At the zendo, people sit along the walls and face out. In Meeting, people will rise and speak sometimes. In the zendo, it is totally silent for 50 minutes. Quakers here meet for worship on Sunday morning and Tuesday evening. The zazen sessions are six days a week.

I really like the similarities and the contrast. I still try to get to the zendo once a week, but it is hard to make the time. I still fall far short from our Quaker testimony on living a simple and unhurried life!

Your over-worked friend.......................Lily

〰〰〰〰〰〰〰〰〰〰〰〰〰〰〰〰〰〰〰〰〰〰〰〰〰〰

Hafeez

Dear Marla,

Wonderful, wonderful that you have found Hafeez and made yourself a tiny corner in your little suite for reading in a contemplative way. How wonderful to read the Islamic poets in an Islamic country, perhaps with the *muezzin* calling people to prayer in the background.

Oh, gosh, girl, thanks for reminding me of these delightful verses. I've scrounged around in boxes until I found my Hafeez volume and brought it up from the cellar. I needed this!

Does the collection you found have the wonderful one that starts

Now is the time to know
That all that you do is sacred.

Now, why not consider
A lasting truce with yourself and God.

Now is the time to understand
That all your ideas of right and wrong
Were just a child's training wheels
To be laid aside
When you can finally live
With veracity
And love.

Is this too modern a translation (Landinsky), talking about "training wheels" and all – they hardly had those in 1360!

What about Rumi and his Sufi love letters to God? Have you got them, too? Do you think they were really letters to a human lover? At least sometimes?

Or is it that love-making at its best is divine for these guys? Why not, after all? I agree.

More soon, after I've read more of these ecstatic, wise poems.

Happily yours...........................*Lily*

~~~~~~

Spoken ministry

Dear compatriot in the realm of seeking and pondering,

Someone rose during the silence during Meeting for Worship today and said that for weeks, a single line from the twenty-third psalm had been resounding in his mind: "I will fear no evil."

He said it again -- "I will fear no evil" -- and sat down. No long speech about what this might mean in our lives. He just sat down. I got goose-pimples. For that moment, it felt as though everyone in the room was sharing that shiver of, what? -- of recognition.

Slowly my heart slowed down and I began thinking about it. Variations offered themselves in my head. *I will not be afraid. The greatest thing we have to fear is fear itself. Fear arises from attachment. Fear is the opposite of faith.*

After a while, as I was beginning to expect, another speaker rose to complete the original line. "I will fear no evil, for the Lord is with me. His rod and his staff, they comfort me."

I wouldn't use quite these words any more. Still, I know that whereas I used to be able to "ask the Lord" to relieve my anxieties, even now I can sit in silence, breathing deep, intending to restrain my ego and calm my soul. There is a slightly different feel to it, but the effect on my agitated psyche is just about the same.

There are huge concepts to ponder here: what evil really is, why fear arises so often, whether it is always in the end the fear of dying, whether fear of death is mostly about the loss of ego.....

Yours...........................Lil

~~~~~~

Revert to belief

Dear Marla,

I appreciate so much your good hope for me that I will be open to the possibility of believing again in God if ever I should be in dire spiritual need. When I was first losing my faith, I used to pray just that. "Dear God in whom I no longer believe, please restore me to faith if times get tough!"

But nowadays I am trying to think about it a bit differently, though I haven't mastered the change yet. Look how I used the words "faith" and "belief" interchangeably in that first paragraph. Buddhist author Sharon Salzburg suggests that they are quite different, and that I can still have faith when I have given up my beliefs. She says "beliefs try to make a known out of an unknown" and relieve our fears. Faith acknowledges and trusts in the ever-changing flow of life."

Well, I am confused about all this still, but I do think I have faith that things will be all right. I don't have much hope for the long-term future of human life on the planet, but even our elimination could be all right, in a sense, you know? I mean, who are we, in the huge over-all sweep of universal time, that our society should survive in its current form? It doesn't matter, really, how things change. Is that a blasphemous thing to say?

I still often actively seek the Holy Spirit, that sense of peace and communion.

I do expect the old maternal prayer to rise as fast as ever to my lips if need arises: "Oh, God, save my baby!"

I still use the old words of praise readily: "How lovely is thy dwelling place, oh Lord of hosts." Admiring the world and its people is a huge part of my practice.

You are among those I admire! Where do you stand among all these conundrums?

Your ever-seeking friend.....................Lillian

Old women

Oh, Marla, thanks for telling me about your ancient friend Sarah, and about your grandmother.

Yes, I, too, have known wise old women. I, too, began to seek them out when I understood that my own mother was not going to be able to offer what I was looking for. Yes, in my case they have mostly been Quakers -- not, I am sure, because Quakers are wiser, but because they are the ones I've had a chance to know.

Mildred is the one who confessed that she was angry at her husband for "abandoning her" when he died – I've thought of that so many times since then. She is the one who urged me to read *I Heard the Owl Call My Name* when we had been talking about mortality and intimations of approaching death. I was in my thirties, she in her eighties.

Another wise old woman, not a Quaker, played part of the Verdi *Requiem* for me, and said she would die one day to the sound of those trumpets calling from the four corners of heaven. I was only about nine at the time, and I was thrilled that she would share such ideas with me.

I've known three women and one man, all well over eighty, who followed the guidance of the Hemlock

Society and managed the timing of their own deaths. I've also known several others who talked about it, but in the end couldn't overcome the instinct to resist to the last breath that Man with the Sickle.

I was introduced to Jungian philosophy and all its complex overlap with religion by an ancient lady who was a wise advisor to several young people in their forties and fifties.

I knew another old woman who was disappointed that she was not seen as a wise mentor and confidant by younger people, though she yearned to be one.

(Gosh, Marla, I haven't laid out the list like this before…..)

I knew a man in his eighties who was still struggling with his relationship with his mother, with problems that were never resolved before her death.

One old correspondent wrote me two letters a week for a couple of years and impressed upon me the understanding that sometimes the major burden of old, old age is suffering a lot of little "miseries" that, added together, make life less and less desirable. This lady, without apparently being aware of it, twice sent me the same lovely card that showed a green lawn disappearing into a lake and forest. When I got the first, I knew right away that she was dying. With the second, I felt she wanted to be sure I understood. It was the last note I ever received from her.

One more, Marla. Once I asked an old Chinese immigrant if he was happy here in America. He searched my face for a moment in silence, then said that happiness was not something that the Chinese took into consideration. I understood him to think it was a preoccupation only of the immature.

I haven't thought of these riches in this way before. Thanks for priming the pump.

Cheers...................Lillian

~~~~~~

Clearness committees

Hi, Marla, to pick up a previous thread, one thing I was wondering was whether Jeremy had a clearness committee in his Meeting in advance of the big changes he made in his life.

He might not have because he made his decision before he was active in the Meeting.

He might not have because he felt absolutely clear already.

He might not have because he thought the issue too complex for Friends in his Meeting to deal with.

He might not have because he didn't feel he could deal with the kind of testing questions a clearness committee would be likley to ask, even though they would be gentle.

But if he did ask for such a committee, and the Oversight Committee felt the Meeting was up to it, Oversight would have assigned a group of three or four Friends to meet with him. Their task would not be to understand and advise on the procedures he was contemplating. Their role would have been to help test whether he was totally clear, in mind and spirit, about going forward. In Quaker lingo, they would "test his leading," help him discern whether his plan was divinely led, and whether the "way was open."

Really, when I think of it, such clearness committees are one of the greatest services we Quakers offer to one another. Maybe the pastor would do it in a conventional church. In our circles, participating in such committees draws all concerned closer into the community. In my Meeting recently, various people have had clearness committees about 1) quitting a job in order to go to Seminary, 2) joining a peace team in Colombia, 3) moving to the East Coast, 4) getting divorced.

We also have clearness committees for membership and marriage. Friends really like being on such committees where people reveal their souls. As you can imagine, it is more gratifying than serving on the budget committee! Of course there are hazards, as when these untrained volunteers do not rightly understand the limits of their role, and verge over into offering advice or pop psychology.

Lots of times, though, people just reach clearness for a big decision on their own or within their family. It means that they check to see whether a pending decision makes sense rationally, will not be harmful to their nearest and dearest, and feels capital R Right in their bones. Often we say we are checking to see whether the decision is led by God.

In Jeremy's case, whether or not a clearness committee was involved in his big decision tells us something about how involved his Meeting is. Here in Santa Carla, decisions like Jeremy's were made before we were told about it, and our task was simply to support the Friend and, in some case, his or her spouse.

See how I still cannot stop thinking about him, bless his heart. Imagine what it must be like.......

Cheers..........................Lillian

I told Jeremy that Lil had written to me about clearness committees, but I did not feel I could ask him if he had had one, and he did not say. It felt most comfortable to just keep up our friendly conversations without any break caused by his revelation.

Activism

Dear Marla, yes, your Jeremy is right when he says that Quakers are no longer as (visibly) active in reform efforts for peace and justice as once upon a time. Quakers played major roles in ending slavery, closing down dungeon-like prisons, establishing mental hospitals, practicing conscientious objection to war, and fighting racism. For challenging the authorities on such issues, over two or three centuries, our forefathers suffered persecution, penalty, and prison.

It is true that we are not very radical and we are not suffering persecution any longer. Probably one reason is that, partly due to Quaker efforts, the penalties for challenging the establishment are not as great these days. Another is that, while old time Quakers made their living by farming or commerce, and could push for peace and justice only in their spare time, many Quakers nowadays are able to spend their whole working lives in jobs that focus on social reform and service. (Viz Jeremy himself.) A third is that much of our political activity is publicly invisible, exerted via letters, petitions and the Internet, rather than by demonstrations and public protests.

But it is probably also true that most of us are so preoccupied with getting food on the table, raising children in challenging environments, and keeping our emotional balance in an overly complex world that we don't have much time or energy for reform activities.

Still, almost all Quakers continue to oppose all wars, all

use of guns, all capital punishment. We continue to support efforts to end racism, sexism, homophobia, and injustices of every kind. We give away a lot of money to progressive service organizations and lobbying groups. We engage in interfaith study and cooperation with the intention that religious hatreds and wars should cease. Our meetinghouses are open to all comers as long as their behavior does not disrupt our community and worship. We constantly review our testimonies on peace, service, integrity, and the rest, and we try to live up to them every hour of every day.

Do I sound defensive here? It is because I sometimes share Jeremy's sense that Friends are not as fervent and involved as they once were. So I am defending them/us against my own criticism! Life is complicated.

So what's happening about Jeremy's departure? Isn't it coming soon? It will be hard for you.....

Love.........................Lily

~~~~~~

Pastoral care

Dear Marla,

Here I am, just home from a couple of "pastoral care" visits. Without any paid clergy, we have to minister to our own shut-ins and elders. It is easier for me than many others because I've had hospice training and experience. I've read a lot about death and dying; to me, it seems deeply related to living a spirit-led life. Are you comfortable in this arena? I think of death as a sacrament, and of attending a death as an experience as holy as a birth, though less exciting. It isn't scary to me.

Anyway, I like old people, even when they are fragile and frail. They are not always nice, though, so I also have much admiration for the hard-pressed staff in the nursing homes I am always visiting.

People often think that caring for incontinence is the hardest task. But I think that the biggest challenge is dealing with the paranoia which makes some patients accuse and malign perfectly honest, hard-working nurses' aides. These aides are mostly immigrant women with tough problems to deal with in their own homes. They are responding to some of the most challenging needs in our society, for minimum wage and marginal benefits. To get blamed for stealing as well – how do they maintain their equanimity?!

And then, of course, one of them will decide she may as well be hung for a wolf as a lamb (how does that expression go?) and she'll pinch a little something after all.

I've climbed on a soap box, haven't I? Sorry. I am jumping off right now.

Your social advocate friend...........................Lily

Death and dying

Oh, yes, Marla, the Tibetan Buddhists are of course another great resource when it comes to thinking positively about death.

Also, there is the stunning concept I once heard a Quaker teacher offer: that the real original sin is getting born in the first place.

That is all he said, but I have pondered it for years, and it seems right to me. By getting born, we left the holy Wholeness, the ground of our being, didn't we?

Birth always launches the ego, and it seems to me that ego is at the root of all our problems. Ego torments our lives almost unceasingly, making us proud, greedy, anxious, self-conscious, resentful or miserable much of our time on earth. Right? I need, I want, I feel, I fear!

So dying should be fine! When we die, thank God, we can give up all that fear and frustration, along with the ego itself. I am bemused by people's desire for a life after death, or for reincarnation for the individual ego. Why would you want it, since the ego is the cause of all grief?

What do you think? Probably most Quakers would not agree with me about this. Is Jeremy too young for this topic? Will I change my own views as I get closer to the Pearly Gates (sic)?

Of course, there are also many wonderful things about life on earth, at least for the advantaged. And ego can be controlled, with effort. I certainly am in no hurry to leave!

Girl, no one gets me writing things like this but you! I should have known your philosophy background would mean you'd be interested in this stuff. I am so glad we have connected again after all these years.

Your fond old college classmate..................Lillian

〰〰〰〰〰〰〰〰〰〰〰〰〰〰〰〰〰〰〰〰〰〰〰〰〰〰〰〰〰〰〰〰

Sleep and unconscious #1

Coming up out of sleep, when light begins to infiltrate behind my eye lids, I sometimes wish I could hit some kind of save button which would protect the half-thought ideas from the dissolution of day light. Do you know what I mean?

Or maybe I need a "merge" command of some sort that would put my conscious mind into the half light of the unconscious where more profound concepts can begin to become visible. Our daily lives are mostly so superficial.

I visit my elderly friends and ask all the old questions – what have you been doing, what are you reading? But perhaps I should be asking what they are now refusing to do and whether they delight in lying around <u>not</u> reading anything.

Shouldn't we, at a certain age, become again like the child with nothing to do but lie on the warm grass watching how the blue of the sky dips and swirls as clouds and birds and imaginary creatures sail past her eyes, be they opened or closed?

I am ready to be someone new, someone who isn't doing something every minute of the day and half the night. Sixty years of habitual busy-ness hold me back, but I aspire to start lying around doing nothing soon!

All these years, the hardest query for me in *Faith and Practice* has been this one: "Do I keep my life uncluttered with things and activities, avoiding commitment beyond my strength and light?"

I don't have too many things, really, and they are all simple and mostly acquired second hand. But I always have too many commitments. I feel in debt to the universe because, compared to most human lives, mine has been blessed. I want to be sure I don't cheat by downplaying my strength and light. You know, like the serenity prayer: I don't want to let laziness or selfishness limit my "courage to change the things I can."

Sounds pretty virtuous, huh? Maybe the real truth is that I am just greedy for involvement and experience.

What about you? What next when you go back to

Tucson? Any new adventure on the horizon?

Yours…………………….Lil

This phenomenon of half-sleep has been of much interest to me lately, so I wrote back promptly.

〰〰〰〰〰〰〰〰〰〰〰〰〰〰〰〰〰〰〰〰〰〰〰〰〰〰〰

Sleep and unconscious #2

Oh, Marla, of course you are right to point out that our rising up from sleep is more or less the opposite from centering down into meditation.

There is a point below daytime consciousness and above night-time sleep where we want to rest, refresh ourselves, and be receptive to "the still, small voice of God," sometimes also thought of as our own deepest insights. Silence and darkness (or at least closed eyes) facilitate us in getting there. We can get to this place as we are coming up from sleep, or as we are in going down into meditation.

Mmmmm, lovely to share these ideas with you.

Yours………………..Lil

〰〰〰〰〰〰〰〰〰〰〰〰〰〰〰〰〰〰〰〰〰〰〰〰〰〰〰

Psychotic

Oh, dear, Marla, this is going to be another post-Meeting letter.

Today there was a hard incident. We want so much to be patient, tolerant, loving – but there are limits. We need to maintain a safe place for people to worship.

A foul-mouthed, bad-smelling psychotic got in past the welcoming committee people who also serve as gentle guards at the door of our inner-city church. It was hard

It wasn't during worship itself, thank heavens – she sat quietly with us. But during the coffee hour afterwards, she started going off in a loud voice about "all the f-ing gay men you have in here who rape all the women...."

Huh? Unclear on the concept!

She went on and on, and started pacing around. So parents swept kids under their wings, other Friends moved away towards the protection of the kitchen, and members of the Ministry and Oversight Committee, who are responsible for controlling scenarios like this, started circling around the poor crazy woman. We've rehearsed for situations like this, and we have a professional or two among us. We gently talked the woman down a bit and moved her out the front door. We let her take the coffee cup with her, but she slammed it to smithereens on the sidewalk as she stalked off, muttering loudly.

It took a while for the adrenalin to drain away. We were especially eager to check in with Ben from the committee, who is gay and could have been stung by the homophobic insults. He was mellow. We were all OK. Even if we had a paid minister, we told each other, we'd have had to help deal with this.

But the poor woman from the street. What about the divine spark in her? There was nothing substantive we could do for her. She rejected our neighborhood resource list, but we are still hoping she'll get hooked up with one of the many local support services. Her situation makes me grieve.

I'll do another letter later to answer your last.

Thanks, good friend.....................Lily

~~~~~~

Small Meetings easier?

Dear Marla,

Yes, Jeremy is right that small-town Meetings may not have trouble with unknown psychotics coming in off the street as often as we do in the cities.

But Friends every where set themselves up for these disturbances by being so welcoming and tolerant. Many Meetings have regular attenders whose behavior is always right on the brink of being socially unacceptable. We consider it part of our practice to extend ourselves as far as we can to accommodate such people. The hard part is that we often disagree among ourselves about how much disturbance we can absorb without jeopardizing the well-being of the Meeting as a whole.

It's the same in other churches, class rooms, and service organizations, right? Who's your most difficult client? Who has been kicked out of the program for disruptive behavior? It's the hardest part of the job to make such decisions, right?

"Never promised you a rose garden," as the song goes!

Cheers.............................Lily

~~~~~~

Born again

Dear Marla,

I was so glad to hear that you got a chance to go up to Lahore, first because it meant a break from work, and second, because all the history of the British Raj in Pakistan is focused there, as I remember it.

Gosh, I majored in history, you might remember, but I feel that I have never really connected the incorrigible passing of historical time with the inevitable passing of my own!

I have another piece to tell in the saga of my coming out as a non-theist in my Meeting.

Not that I am very far out yet; I am still nervous about distressing people, especially those who are becoming more Christocentric as I am moving in the other direction.

But I had a new "opening" the other day when someone told me that one of our more Christ-centered people is feeling deeply centered and blessed by his faith. Apparently Jason shyly told our mutual friend that he really is feeling "born again" in his faith in Christ. Seems like Jason is as hesitant about declaring himself at that end of the continuum as I am on the other.

My reaction was to be very happy for him. I had to think hard about why. I guess, because I know how deeply some of us struggle to find a faith stance that works for us, I am glad for anybody who has found a religious position that feels right. He or she can *rest* there for a while, you know what I mean? We all need these times of rest and confidence.

Anyway, Sandy urged me to tell Jason directly that I had heard this news about him, and that I was glad for him. So I did that today, as simply as I could, and Jason received it simply. I think we both felt a little glow of "the Light."

Your happy friend..............Lily

~~~~~~

Getting more Christ-centered

Dear Marla,

Well, yes, I do know of four or five long-time "weighty" Quakers who are becoming more Christo-centric with the years. I don't know exactly what they are believing, though, or how they apply their beliefs to the problems of daily life.

I know that many atheist Americans tend to think of belief in Christianity as a lower rung on some kind of spiritual ladder. I did, for a while. Do you? I've come to think we run the risk of arrogance with such ranking. There are areas of understanding that are not entirely rational and are not accessible to some smart people, fortunate as they may be in the acuity of their intellect.

Raised on the good old notion that all men are created equal, I have finally figured out that we are not all created equal in every respect, though the divine spark is alive (bright or only smoldering) in all of us. I've come to believe that the wisest man is the one who best uses the resources he has been given, to live the best life he can. To some it is given to find strength in religious faith, to others it is not.

I can't imagine that Christianity and the other major religions would have lasted so long if they did not have a substantial evolutionary value. Religious belief keeps anxiety at bay and makes us stronger and more persevering, don't you think? Yes, you do, because this is more or less what you offered to me in the language of transactional analysis a while back. Yes, yes.

Cheers, dear.........................Lil

~~~~~~

Friends Church

Really, Marla, this is the most unusual, more-or-less three-way exchange! It is so fun and funny and unexpected that you should be in the middle of this conversation about Quakers with Jeremy (over dinners) and me (by e-mail).

Jeremy is right that a Quaker Church, aka "Pastoral Meeting," tends to be more Christ-centered than any "unprogrammed," silent Meeting with no pastor.

But there is space for us all. It's like me, still hanging with my silent Meeting as I become a post-theist. If a Friend "finds Christ" or is "born again" after ten or twenty or even thirty years in an unprogrammed, silent Meeting, s/he is not going to leave for a pastoral Friends Church. Well, some do, but it is not required. Primarily we are seekers. We support one another in seeking and finding what rings true for each of us. As long as it includes the concept that there is a divine spark worthy of nurture in every single person on the planet.

It is true that Richard Nixon was for a time a member of a Friends (Quaker) Church in Whittier, California. In my circle of Friends, we were embarrassed by his politics, but respectful of his religion.

By the way, encouraged by this exchange with you (and with Jeremy through you), I mentioned to another friend that my hero was that "anti-Establishment radical, Jesus of Nazareth." She challenged me. She said that though Jesus threw the tax collectors out of the temple and stood up to Pontius Pilate, being an anti-Establishment rebel was only a secondary claim to fame.

She said Jesus was really more notable as an advocate for diversity and inclusion. She pointed out that he welcomed the Samaritan (was there a race issue there?) and healed the sick and disabled. He worked with poor fishermen, and called the children to himself. He talked to Martha as a thoughtful equal, and let Mary Magdalene comfort him in the way any prostitute would.

Well, all the more reason to follow his lead with conviction, I thought, if you don't feel "washed in the blood of the Lamb"!

Oh, gosh, it has started to rain and I have got clothes on

the line. Yes, really. I believe in solar-powered drying for my laundry.

Running……………………………..Lil

Our correspondence dropped off here for a while. I was so deeply engaged with life in Karachi that I hardly noticed. But Lillian worried that she had disappointed me.

~~~~~~

Summer slump

Sorry, Marla, I haven't written in a long time, weeks, maybe. I have been in a gloom, probably "seasonal affect disorder" making me s.a.d. For almost a month, in the middle of summer, it has been dreadfully cold and foggy in my neighborhood, and it really gets me down. Sun will come by two pm, maybe, but then it will be cold and foggy again by six.

Also, I am in despair and dismay about the collapsed peace movement. War churns on in Iraq and Afghanistan, but almost no one notices any more. Or people notice, but have no hope of changing things. Even with a strong majority of American voters opposing the war this last year, the government does not change its ways. It feels as though the country has been bought out by the military industrial establishment. It seems as though democracy is crumbling – that is of more concern to me than the war, really. There have always been wars, but never in my time have democratic principles been so flaunted, democratic practices so eroded as during this Bush-Cheney administration.

The sectarian peace movement in this town is in tatters, with turf fights and internal hostilities on every side. The ideological pacifists won't work with the socialists or with the groups willing to shout and swear, break windows and throw things at the cops. The suburbanites don't come into the city for big marches and rallies any more. Liberal cynics are saying that even if Obama wins, he won't be able to fulfill his promises, even if he manages to survive!

Stop me this minute! What is the point of going on and on with complaints? Instead I should be taking comfort in the fact that our senator voted against new military appropriations, a major accomplishment for the peace movement, even though it didn't change the overall vote. I should be glad that our federal representatives urge us to keep the pressure up so that they can say their constituents are demanding change.

At Meeting, a couple of us offer books to read, movies to watch, and petitions to sign. There is little response from Friends. People take more interest in environmental reforms they can implement tangibly in their own homes. Everyone took the free Energy-Star light bulbs we offered, several have bought a hybrid car, many are driving as little as possible. At least two of us use a clothes line. Solar clothes dryer, what a radical concept!

Your clothes, if I remember correctly, are washed by a *dhobi* squatting near a bucket, and dried by being laid flat on the ground for twenty minutes in the sun! I hope so.

I haven't answered any of your questions in this letter, and I'll get to that when I write tomorrow or soon.

Keep up the good work...........................Lily

~~~~~~

Still depressed

Dear friend, my parents always warned, "If you don't have anything nice to say, don't say anything." So I won't write much, as I am still "in the slough of despond." I have written a lot in my journal, a good, hidden place to vent.

Meanwhile, Jeremy's departure must be a downer for you. Has his replacement arrived yet? The constant turn-over is a challenge in such foreign posts, isn't it? Too bad his organization couldn't afford to pay for an overlap, so he could train the new person.

But it is good to think that you may be able to visit him when you also return to the US, that he doesn't live too awfully far away. Will he be with his father at first?

Anyway, more in a day or two, darley. Speaking of journals, our letters back and forth have functioned sort of like journals, haven't they? I've kept them all in my PC files, have you?

Love to you.....................Lily

~~~~~~

Obama campaign

Well, Marla, venting to you, "sitting zazen" at the Zen Center, writing some more in my journal, and talking to a friend-by-phone, I got clear enough to make some decisions, and brave enough to speak to a couple of people about the problems we share. So of course, everything is now looking better! I guess it just takes having the faith to wade through it all! I always remember that Beatles line: "We get by with a little help from our friends!" Plus, the sun is shining a bit more now.

I've figured out a way of talking with others about supporting the Obama campaign, and about how we will respond whether he makes it or not on Election Day. It feels so important to be prepared.

But meanwhile, there you are, far away, off in a strange land. What do people say about the U.S., about Obama, about our election process? Do you have an absentee ballot? PLEASE be sure to vote – every single vote will count. Can you advocate for Obama among Americans there without offending people? As I remember, foreign service people tended to be pretty conservative. But now there are all the NGOs, the service organizations, and so forth. What's the mood in the expatriate community in Karachi?

Colorado is a swing state. You know, it could go Democrat or Republican, who knows. So I am thinking of going to Denver to campaign for Obama for a week. Did you ever know Caroline Swanson in our class? I think I could stay with her. What do you think?

Cheers...........................Lily

~~~~~~

Oversight Committee, Election

Oh gosh, Marla, sometimes it surely seems that it would be easier to have some sort minister in charge of our congregation. Last night I spent four hours at an oversight committee meeting, trying with great care to figure out how to handle a challenging and unforgiving attender in a gentle and loving way. It takes a lot of effort and self discipline.

We are welcoming to people of every sort, but not to behaviors of every kind. When an individual's behavior is repeatedly disrupting silent worship or group sharing sessions, the oversight committee just has to curb it somehow, for the sake of the whole

Meeting. But of course we try not to hurt the offending individual any more than necessary.

Some people catch on quickly to the idea of "having a divine leading." It takes longer to understand the concept of "testing your leading" among Friends. This is the crucial piece which keeps us from getting led astray by our own enthusiasms, as we have tried to explain to this attender at Meeting.

The larger group may agree it is a leading for you, but not for the rest of them. For example, just because you are "led" to be a war tax resister doesn't mean that you should be pushy in urging other Friends to do the same thing. It does not mean you should flaunt your own virtue. The sense of being led does not always mean that you are "rightly led."   Other Friends may feel that your leading is misguided and want to "labor with you" about it. But on the other hand, they could be wrong, possibly because they are conventional and conservative old fuddy duddies!

So this is what we were dealing with last night. It was a long hard meeting -- and also a prime example of Quakers at their best, seeking to solve a community problem in as caring a way as possible.

Meanwhile, we are all reeling with the news of Sarah Palin as a vice presidential candidate. What do people in Pakistan say about these dramatic and bizarre American politics? I got into a dreadful funk about it Sunday, actually sat and cried. Democracy is totally bankrupt when a really inappropriate candidate can be put forward by one of the parties, when the military-industrial establishment endorses a puppet, knowing they won't let him/her make any decisions even if s/he wins.

My response to dismay, you might guess by now, is to figure out some action to take. If it accomplishes nothing else, it makes me feel as though I tried. So I really am going to Denver for a week, to help with the Obama campaign there.

I'd love to know what you read these days in the Pakistani papers and hear in the corridors at work. Or do you think your Pakistani co-workers are too polite to criticize the US system in your presence?

More later, maybe not 'til after Denver.

Your compulsive activist friend.....................Lily

~~~~~~

Debriefing Denver campaign

I am in a whirl, Marla, with 113 e-mails to answer and all kinds of catch-up to do. I am reporting back to different people and groups about my week in Denver. I only have time now to tell you my favorite episode in the week.

I spent a lot of time in front of a huge WalMart store, checking if people were registered to vote. One bent old black woman with a walker grinned broadly at me, and said,

"Honey, Ah'm registered and mah children are registered and mah grand-children are registered, and all forty nine of us are going to vote for that man on that special Tuesday!"

Coming back by train through the gorges of the Rocky Mountains was absolutely wonderful. If you have never taken that trip, find an excuse to do it sometime. Come see me in California!

First you'll have to get back to the US. You'll have the same culture shock Jeremy is reporting; I remember how it was. We Americans all have so much too much in the way of things and choices in our lives. You'll get back the week after the election, I gather.
Maybe we'll have a fine, intelligent, educated new president-elect and things will change. How will you be involved, do you think?

Gotta run, darley, too much to do.

Cheers............................Lily

~~~~~~

Obama victory

Hallelujah! Hip hip hooray! It feels here as though everyone is celebrating and glad. People were literally dancing in the streets here last night. Young black men have a whole new look to them; their world view has shifted.

I am so delighted that I can hardly sit down. No matter what happens after this (as long as they don't kill him), this has been an enormous victory, a huge step forward in race relations for the world. My half-black daughter is ecstatic. Understandably, it is Michele Obama she identifies with and keeps talking about.

Meanwhile, you are back! Probably in culture shock. How is all this election fervor in Tucson? I suppose the happy liberals are celebrating in circles well away from the dismayed conservatives.

For me, there are two big hopes. One is that Obama will return us to the true principles of democracy. The other is that Obama will turn us away from war and the outrageous financial costs of a foreign policy based on violence.

I know being hopeful has a flip side, being fearful – that he won't be able to do these things. I know that being hopeful is a form of grasping onto what I want. I don't care! I'm gonna grasp, at least for a while! And I'm going to keep working at it. After all, what he said was, *Yes, we can!*

I'm tickled that you visited Tucson Friends Meeting. Sorry that Jeremy and I forgot to tell you that people mostly just wear everyday clothes – no suits or high heels or makeup -- and are very informal. Yes, that burst of coffee-hour conversation after the worship and announcements is kind of a shock at first, isn't it? Sometimes I just sit still and watch the others for a while, before I get up. I tend to feel pretty loving towards people right at that moment.

And now you are going to have a reunion with Jeremy, and go to his small-town Meeting in Tannerville. Gosh, you're taking the full-immersion course in Quakerism, aren't you? How long a drive is it? I can't wait to hear all about it.

Glad you feel renewed by the long absence in your relations to your kids. A Thanks-giving reunion will be good. I'll anchor the Meeting Thanksgiving here again this year, as is my custom (because my kids are so far away). Members and attenders and their friends who are at loose ends that day come together at eleven in the morning for worship first, then share the usual Thanksgiving fare, with everyone bringing something. I always messed up the turkey when my kids were young, but I have more or less mastered it for these Meeting gatherings. ☺

Remember *L'Enfance du Christ* from school? My rule and ritual is that I can start on Christmas music after Thanksgiving dinner, so my plans for that evening include Christmas carols and *L'Enfance.*

Enjoy it all, dear friend.

Cheers…………………………...Lil

Meeting Jeremy's father

Dear Marla,

I'm glad to hear that your visit to Tannerville went so
well. Your comments about how different Meeting was
there from the one in Tucson were perceptive, but not
surprising to me. For all that Friends Meetings
everywhere have substantial similarities, the difference
in size affects all aspects of a Meeting's life. Many
Quakers prefer a small Meeting. In any case, it is
always a treat for long-time Quakers to visit Meetings
other than their own. Provides affirmation and
perspective.

I agree that it is especially commendable that so small a
Meeting in so conservative a state has apparently
worked through most of the challenges of Jeremy's
gender change together. This is hard stuff for people to
cope with.

And if it was hard for the Meeting, think of Jeremy's
parents! How great that you got a chance to see him
with his father. What a treat that they took you to
lunch with them. I loved how you described their ease
together – and how you also thought you saw the
father (what's his name?) watching his son with
curiosity and delight. He must have gotten quite a kick
out of hearing you and Jeremy talk together about the
Karachi experience.

I forgot to ask you earlier: does Jeremy attend the Winter Gathering of FLGBTQC? It is named *Friends for Lesbian gay bi trans and queer concerns*, but they call it by the initials! (I think they should simply call it Queer Quakers of America – QQA.) I should think it would be especially valuable for a Quaker trans-man from Arizona, who doesn't have quite the supportive community of the alternately-sexed that is available in the San Francisco Bay Area.

By the way, I had to look up that line of initials at **www.Quaker.org**, and then under Religious Society of Friends. There is a slew of information and a ton of links there.

Well, darley, now that the election furor and follow-up is over, I am resolved to get back to serious writing. So ta-ta for now.

Cheers..................Lily

~~~~~~

Visit planned

Girl, only you of all my girlfriends manages to keep on sparking little flames of interest in guys of a certain age!

How did Jeremy get a father with a French name: Claude? Claude Anderson, of all things. Did Claude have a French mother?

Of course, I am delighted to hear that he comes to Tucson for work from time to time and has suggested lunch.

Of course, he is glad to know more about the woman who was such a friend of his son's in Karachi.

BUT ….. Is there any way you can keep your hopes and expectations in check, so that you will not get disappointed?

Sorry I am such a cynic. Have a wonderful time with him!

Love…………………….Lily

~~~~~~

Book idea

Marla, gosh, you have caught me totally off guard with the idea that my letters could become the substance of a book about modern Quaker life and concerns. Did you know before your lunch date that Claude Anderson was a production editor? Is this for real or do you just want an excuse to see more of him? (Well, if so, that's OK, too!)

But, yikes, did you show all those letters to him unexpurgated? Didn't I talk somewhere about uncomfortable bras and dry skin in private regions of the body? I suppose, as an experienced production editor, he will calmly red pencil any such passages without a blink. I guess that's the kind of thing we are supposed to edit out now.

Are you sure it should be just my letters, not yours as well? What about excerpts from both?

Did you tell Jeremy about the idea? Is he OK with it? Given the way his story is featured, do we need to disguise his identity, or anyone else's?

Wow, this is a challenge. Go ahead and try it. Will you let me see your draft before you send it to Claude?

Please tell Claude he can call me if he wants to. I'll call you tomorrow, too, to talk about this more.

Cheers…………………………………..Lily

About the Author

Elizabeth Boardman has been an active and involved Quaker for more than fifty years. Her father was a conscientious objector assigned to work in the War Relocation Authority camps for four years when she was an infant. He and her mother joined the Religious Society of Friends when Elizabeth was twelve.

Elizabeth herself joined Cambridge Meeting (Massachusetts) just before her marriage at age 19, and has belonged to three California Monthly Meetings since 1965. Elizabeth developed and managed services for frail elders for thirty years, and was a founder of Friends House, a Quaker retirement community in Santa Rosa, California.

A committed political activist, mother and grandmother, Elizabeth's earlier books include *Taking a Stand: A Guide to Peace Teams and Accompaniment Projects* (2005); *Where Should I Stand? A Field Guide for Monthly Meeting Clerks* (2008); and a book of stories about San Francisco called *I'm Not a Tourist, I Live Here!* (2011).

Made in the USA
Charleston, SC
06 January 2013